REVISED & UPDATED

COACHING YOUTH
SOCCER

REVISED & UPDATED

COACHING YOUTH SOCCER

SECOND EDITION

The Guide for Coaches, Parents and Athletes

John P. McCarthy, Jr.

FOREWORD BY HEATHER MITTS,
Gold Medalist, U.S. Women's National Team

INTRODUCTION BY NEEL SHAH,
Fan Development Manager,
Major League Soccer

BETTERWAY BOOKS
Cincinnati, Ohio

Other fine Betterway Books are available from your local bookstore or direct from the publisher.

11 10 09 08 07   5 4 3 2 1

Distributed in Canada by Fraser Direct, 100 Armstrong Avenue, Georgetown, ON, Canada L7G 5S4, Tel: (905) 877-4411. Distributed in the U.K. and Europe by David & Charles, Brunel House, Newton Abbot, Devon, TQ12 4PU, England, Tel: (+44) 1626 323200, Fax: (+44) 1626 323319, E-mail: postmaster@davidandcharles.co.uk. Distributed in Australia by Capricorn Link, P.O. Box 704, Windsor, NSW 2756 Australia, Tel: (02) 4577-3555.

Library of Congress Cataloging-in-Publication Data

McCarthy, John P., 1947-
 Coaching youth soccer : the guide for coaches, parents, and athletes / by John P. McCarthy, Jr. -- 2nd ed.
    p. cm.
 Rev. ed. of: A parent's guide to coaching soccer. c1990.
 Includes index.
 ISBN-13: 978-1-55870-794-8 (pbk. : alk. paper)
 ISBN-10: 1-55870-794-8 (pbk. : alk. paper)
 1. Soccer for children--Coaching. I. McCarthy, John P., 1947- Parent's guide to coaching soccer. II. Title.

 GV943.8.M36 2007
 796.334083--dc22
 2006033546

Edited by Michelle Ehrhard
Designed by Grace Ring
Illustrations by John Rizzo
Cover design by Sean Braemer and Claudean Wheeler
Page layout by Eric West
Cover photography by Christine Polomsky
Production coordinated by Mark Griffin

F+W PUBLICATIONS, INC.

ABOUT THE AUTHOR

Jack McCarthy, like many Americans, is a sports enthusiast and has played and coached numerous sports all of his life. As a parent, and now grandparent, he knows that athletic competition builds self-confidence in young people. It also prepares them to handle life's challenges and teaches them how to succeed. The Betterway Coaching Kids series was developed by Jack to help parents and coaches ensure that their child's experience in sports is a positive one.

Jack is an attorney and works for the New Jersey Courts. He lives with his wife and family, which includes three children and four grandchildren, in Hillsborough, New Jersey. His other books in the series include titles on baseball, basketball, and football. He has also written *Baseball's All-Time Dream Team*.

DEDICATION

To Mike Christy for suggesting I coach; to Bob Walsh and John MacIvor for coaching with me; to Roy Dyer for his advice; to the boys and girls and parents who hung in there through the rain, mud, heat, and cold; to my daughter Michelle, son Joey, and granddaughter Shannan; and to the spirit that moves all of us to challenge life. This book is ours!

ACKNOWLEDGMENTS

Special thanks to photo models Kristine, Shannan, and Connor McCarthy, Max Henig, Kyle Shannon, and Tucker Sandercock.

TABLE OF CONTENTS

FOREWORD

By Heather Mitts, Gold Medalist, U.S. National Women's Soccer Team

Learning the fundamentals of any sport at an early age is an important part of a child's development. Team sports, such as soccer, build relationships, instill confidence, and hone the competitive spirit.

Parents and coaches of young boys and girls can be role models by following the rules of the game and emphasizing fair play. I hope that everyone using this book will realize the impact they could have on young athletes' lives.

And remember, the most important thing is to have fun!

INTRODUCTION

By Neel Shah, Fan Development Manager, Major League Soccer

I have many fond memories of my childhood in Huntington Beach, CA, but none stick out more than my first season of youth soccer. I remember it all so well: meeting my teammates for the first time, getting my uniform, scoring my first goal, eating oranges at halftime, and, of course, snacks after the game. I remember having the time of my life without even realizing that I was growing mentally and physically. I look back now and can admit that I had fallen in love with this sport before I even knew what love was. I have since gone on to play soccer at various levels domestically and internationally and have now made a career out of creating soccer-playing opportunities for kids while promoting Major League Soccer.

My passion for soccer can be traced back to the dedication of one individual. My parents are from India and they dreamed of providing me with an "American" childhood. My best friend's dad, Mr. Moore, caught on to this and signed me up for the PeeWee Soccer team he was coaching. He wasn't a top-level coach by any means; he was just a kind parent whose objective was to let us have fun while teaching us the basics of the game. He worked hard at learning the sport himself so that he could teach us how to play well. He ended up coaching me during my first four years of soccer and I am confident that during that time he had no idea what kind of impact he was making on so many of our lives.

Coaching Youth Soccer is a "must read" for anyone looking to make the same of kind impact through this sport. This book will provide you with the fundamentals you need to know to effectively teach soccer and, more importantly, provide kids with a positive environment where they can have fun and achieve personal growth. It takes you step by step through all of the fundamentals and teaching progressions that are essential to improving skill level and knowledge of the game. It even provides a comprehensive soccer glossary and advice on proper actions during games.

Just by opening this book you have taken the first step in enriching young people's lives through this sport. I applaud your interest and dedication to this cause and truly hope that you enjoy your experience coaching youth soccer.

THE GAME OF SOCCER

HISTORY

Soccer is a very old sport. Legends tell of barbarian soldiers kicking around the skulls of their enemies. The earliest evidence of the game was found in a Chinese military manual in the third century B.C. However, it's likely that kids were kicking round objects as soon as there were kids and round objects. For the last one thousand years, the game has flourished in England. It was initially played between two towns kicking a pig's bladder from a point midway between the towns. Hundreds of people played at one time, and it often became violent. Some rules were eventually formulated, but not until about 1850. One day a player picked up the ball and ran with it, leading to the formation of rugby, and, still later, American-style football.

To most of the world, the game Americans call soccer is known as football. It is clearly the most popular game in the world. Over 130 nations are now members of F.I.F.A. (the Fédération Internationale de Football Association), the world soccer governing body. Soccer became an Olympic sport in 1908, but the true pinnacle of soccer is the World Cup. Since 1930, every four years each nation sends a team of its citizens to vie for the trophy. Teams from Brazil, Italy, Argentina, and Germany have dominated the world stage, while stars such as Pelé, Franz Beckenbauer, Diego Maradona, and David Beckham have taken the game to its highest levels.

In colonial America during the 1620s, the Pilgrims played a form of soccer, which the Indians called *pasuckquakkohwog*, meaning, "they come together to play ball with the foot." By the 1820s, many American colleges played the sport. The United States was granted membership in F.I.F.A. in 1914. The United States Soccer Federation (U.S.S.F.) is the current ruling body for American soccer. American women's soccer has been dominant for decades, with the national women's team winning the first-ever women's World Cup in 1991, Olympic Gold in 1996 and 2004, and the women's World

3

Cup again in 1999. Stars like Mia Hamm, Michelle Akers, and Heather Mitts have inspired young girls, and now over six million girls play soccer in the United States. American men's soccer has continued its strong growth and is slowly becoming competitive on the world stage. U.S. Youth Soccer is a member of U.S.S.F and administers youth soccer in the United States.

A BRIEF DESCRIPTION OF THE SPORT

Two teams of up to eleven players (including the goalie) attempt to score goals by kicking the soccer ball into the opponent's goal net. Goalposts are situated at either end of the football-sized field. Players are assigned to sections of the field and are generally responsible for that area. Some players try to score, and so they play forward into the opponent's territory, and are called *forwards* or *wings*. Some defend and stay back to defend their team's territory, and so are called *fullbacks*. Some play the midfield, and are called just that, *midfielders* or *halfbacks*. A *goalkeeper* or *goalie* plays in the goal box and is the only player who may use his hands to catch or strike the ball. (We'll discuss positions in detail in chapter five.)

A goal is scored when the whole ball is completely past the goal line. Professional games last ninety minutes, with the teams exchanging sides after forty-five minute halves, and a five minute halftime break. Younger kids play shorter games. Play is continuous and the clock is stopped only for unusual delays such as injuries. The game goes on, rain or shine, unless the field becomes hazardous or there is a lightning storm. Rules on substitutes vary. In the pros, teams are limited to three substitutes per game, while at youth levels subs are frequent. With older kids, subs usually come in at the start of the second half or midway through the half. At younger age levels, they are allowed when any referee's whistle stops action or on any out-of-bounds violation.

Players may receive and advance the ball with any part of their bodies except the arms or hands; upper shoulders are okay.

When a player kicks the ball out of bounds on the side of the field, the opposing team may throw the ball back into play from the point it left the field. If a ball is kicked past the out of bounds line behind the goal (the *goal line*) by an offensive player, the opponent's goalie may kick it (*goal kick*) into play from within the area just in front of the goal. If the defense kicks the ball past the goal line, the offense is awarded a direct kick (*corner kick*) from the corner of the field (see pages 55–56).

That's soccer. It's not a complicated game. There are not as many rules as most American sports, nor are there many set "plays," as found in basketball and football.

Its beauty is in its simplicity. Kids get to kick a ball around and try to score, and that's about it. Of course, there are rules limiting physical contact with players and the ball, as well as penalties to keep the game safe.

THE LAWS OF THE GAME

Soccer field play is controlled by a set of seventeen Laws of the Game, as the official rules of F.I.F.A. are named. They were developed in England in 1863 as the first universally accepted rules for soccer. These rules address field dimensions, ball size, number of players, duration of the match, and how to start and restart play, including free, penalty, goal and corner kicks, and throw-ins.

PENALTIES

Much of the focus of soccer rules is on fouls, in an endeavor to keep the game safe for all players. At one time, violence was prevalent on the field. Games were often rumbles between villages, with hundreds of players on each side, and with no rules. It got so bad that King Edward banned games in England in 1314. Thus, the Laws of the Game were primarily motivated by the need to remove violence from the field of play. (Unfortunately, professional soccer has also been associated with fan violence, particularly outside America, demonstrating the passion with which the sport is regarded around the world.)

Upon a foul, the referee may stop play by blowing a whistle. However, if the team that was fouled has possession of the ball, the referee may allow them to continue playing if it is to that team's advantage, rather than to be awarded a free kick.

When play is blown dead, the referee signals whether the penalty award is a *direct kick*, by pointing his hand toward the goal, or an *indirect kick*, by pointing his hand straight up. The referee's other hand usually points to the spot from where the kick must be taken. (See Referee Signals on page 141.)

A direct kick means that the kicker may score by shooting directly at the goal. In an indirect kick, another player must touch the ball before a goal can be scored. Defensive players must stand 10 yards away from the kicker on all free kicks (this distance is shorter in youth play and varies depending on the age of the players). If a direct kick is awarded close to the goal, the defense often forms a human wall to protect the goal.

A *penalty kick* is awarded for a violation that would result in a direct kick from within the *penalty area* (area in front of each goal, explained on page 10). The shot is taken from the penalty mark, a short line 12 yards from the center of the goal (8–10 yards for youth teams). All other players must remain outside the penalty area. The goalie must have both feet on the goal line until the ball is kicked. The kicker or a teammate may take additional shots upon a rebound touched by the goalie (a rebound off the goal post not touched by the goalie is a dead ball).

Direct kicks are awarded upon intentional fouls such as kicking, jumping, striking, tripping, holding, or pushing another player; intentionally touching the ball with the hand (a handball) or arm; and offside. Limited physical contact with the chest, shoulder, or hip (no arms) between players is allowed so long as both of the players are playing the ball.

Indirect kicks are awarded for unintentional fouls, obstruction, or dangerous play, such as raising the foot high, lowering one's head, unsportsmanlike behavior, abusive language, kicking the ball when on the ground, or kicking a ball held by the goalie.

The referee may additionally warn a player or coach by holding a *yellow card* in the air or expel a player or coach from the game by holding a *red card* in the air. Two yellow-card warnings equal a red card. Red cards often carry a suspension for additional games.

The goalie may use his hands in the penalty area. Within this space is the goal area, which is directly in front of the goal posts. Upon catching the ball, the goalie can take only four steps before the ball must then be punted or thrown outside of the penalty area. An exception is made for players under eight; there is no step limit. Once the goalie possesses the ball, it may not be kicked from his hands. He also cannot be interfered with while in the goal area.

OTHER KEY RULES

Offside: Perhaps the most controversial calls in soccer games relate to the offside rule. This rule basically tries to keep players from hanging around the opposing team's goal to get a pass and an easy shot. The general idea is that there must always be either an opponent (other than the goalie) or the ball between an offensive player and the goal. The rule books say that a player is offside if he is nearer the opponent's goal line than the ball is at the moment the ball is played toward the player from a teammate, unless a) the player is on one's own half of the field; b) two defenders (including the goalie) are nearer the goal line than the attacker; c) the offensive player receives the ball on a goal kick, corner kick, throw-in, or drop ball. In other words, if a player doesn't have the ball, there must be a defender (plus the goalie) between him and the goal. You basically have to earn forward progress with the ball. This rule is the source of many a groan at soccer games. It is often missed if there are no linesmen, and some referees ignore or misunderstand the part about not being offside at the time the ball is kicked. Often a player will move past his defender as soon as the ball is in flight and will erroneously be called offside.

Defenders can use this rule effectively to stop forwards from penetrating. If they do not fall back toward the goal, so long as the ball is still upfield, then the players they are covering can't advance beyond them. A good defensive play near the goal is for defenders to all run a few steps forward so the players they are guarding are offside. This is called an *offside trap*. Again, the ball must still be upfield, since all offensive players may advance as far as the ball. We'll review this further in chapter six on defense.

Corner kick: When the ball goes out of bounds past the goal line and was last touched by a defensive player, the opponent is awarded a free direct kick. The ball is placed at the corner of the field nearest to where it went out of bounds. The player kicks the ball hard, just below the center, and tries to place it near the goal. Sometimes a player can curve the ball right into the goal. The other teammates bunch up and charge to the area where the player tries to kick the ball. A tall player might try to "head" the ball into the goal. The defense positions their players at each goal post and other defenders *mark* (cover one-on-one) the forwards as they charge. The goalie must decide whether or not to leap to grab the ball from the air.

Goal kick: A free kick awarded to the defense when an offensive player kicks the ball out of bounds beyond the goal line. The kick must be taken from within the goal area on the same side from which the ball went out of bounds. It must exit the penalty area before any player can play the ball. At young ages, the kick should be to the corner of the penalty area since kicks to the middle carry a high risk of interception by an offensive player in prime scoring position. Sometimes, a goalie kicks it to an unmarked (uncovered) player close to the penalty area perimeter, who then shovels it back to the goalie. The goalie may then punt or throw the ball upfield.

Throw-in: When the ball is kicked out of bounds past the sideline, the team who did not kick it out of bounds is awarded a throw-in. A player throws the ball in from out of bounds. She must hold the ball with two hands over her head and throw it without lifting either leg from the ground. A common violation in youth soccer is to lift the back foot a bit on a *throw-in*. If that happens, the ball is awarded to the opponent for a throw-in.

Advantage: There is a rule that allows a referee to ignore a foul if the fouled team has an advantage, e.g., the fouled player is advancing toward the goal and keeps possession despite the foul.

FIELD DIMENSIONS

Modern soccer is played on a flat field up to 130 yards long and 100 yards wide. American soccer fields are about the size of a football field, 100 yards by 50 yards. Kids play on fields about 80 yards long, and beginners play on fields much smaller. *Small-sided games* often occur with only six or seven players on a side, so smaller fields are marked out. A field needs to be large enough for players to run freely, but not so large that they will tire quickly. At either end of the field is a goal with side posts 24 feet apart holding up a crossbar 8 feet from the ground and backed up by a net. (See figure 1-1 on page 9.)

When I first coached soccer in 1980, we put young children under age ten into full field play, eleven against eleven. That's the way it was done, but it was clear that it was too much for them. I often broke scrimmages into games of six or seven on a side, or even smaller. Soccer was in its infancy in America. Eleven on eleven overwhelms children, and does not build confidence. Children don't get the ball enough, don't develop skills, and often just bunch up into a swarm of stampeding kids. In the 1990s, leagues began fielding teams of eight players for kids under twelve years old, certainly for kids under ten. In 2003, U.S. soccer rules further embraced small-sided games (small fields, fewer players). We'll review this in detail in chapter six.

The current U.S. soccer rules on field sizes accommodate the differences in size, speed, and skill levels for children of different ages. Teams of four and three are recommended for the under eight and under-six age levels, respectively. The under-ten level has seven players on a side, and under-twelve has eight players a side. We'll discuss these differences and others in more detail throughout the book. The recommended field dimensions for kids are as follows:

AGE	LENGTH	WIDTH
Under Twelve	70–90 yards	40–50 yards
Under Ten	45–60 yards	35–45 yards
Under Eight	25–35 yards	20–30 yards
Under Six	20–30 yards	15–25 yards

1-1. FIELD DIMENSIONS

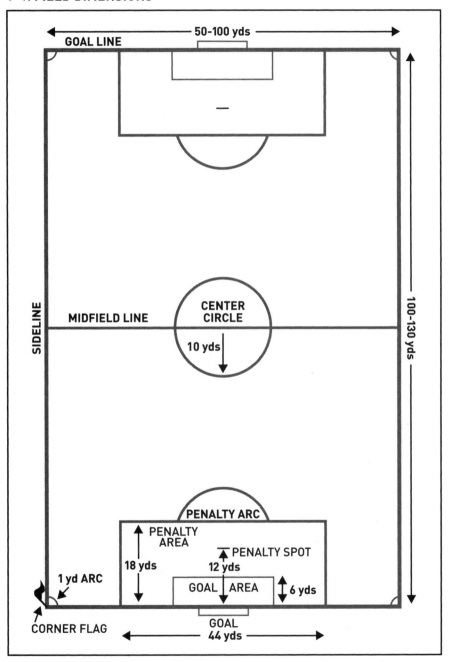

GOAL LINE
50-100 yds
100-130 yds
SIDELINE
MIDFIELD LINE
CENTER CIRCLE
10 yds
PENALTY ARC
PENALTY AREA
PENALTY SPOT
18 yds
12 yds
GOAL AREA
6 yds
1 yd ARC
CORNER FLAG
GOAL
44 yds

1–2. KICKOFF

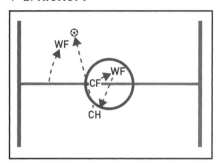

Center forward rolls ball forward to a wing forward (WF), who in turn shovels it back to the center halfback (CH). She then passes it up strongly to the other wing forward.

1–3. SOCCER BALLS

Pictured, for comparison, are a size 5, a size 4, a size 3, and a size 1 soccer ball.

Play begins in the *center circle*, the 10-yard radius circle in the middle of the field, where the ball is placed at the beginning of each half and after each goal. A player rolls the ball forward to a teammate to start play. That player may advance the ball, or he can kick it back to the person who first touched it to set up a more controlled advance. Defenders may not enter the circle until the ball rolls one full turn. (See figure 1-2.)

The *penalty area* is the 18-yard by 44-yard box in front of each goal. For youth soccer it is smaller, 14 yards by 28 yards at the under-twelve and under-ten levels, and there is no penalty box in the under-eight and under-six levels. Penalties in this area lead to a penalty shot. Within this space is the 6-yard by 20-yard goal area directly in front of the goal. No player can interfere with the goalie in the goal area. The goal area for under-twelve and under-ten players is 6 yards by 15 yards. For under-eight players it is 3 yards by 12 yards, and for under-six players there is no goal area (and no goalie!).

SOCCER BALLS

Soccer balls come in three basic sizes: 3, 4, and 5. Size 5 is the official regulation size, 27–28 inches in circumference (about an inch in diameter smaller than a basketball), and 14–16 ounces in weight. Size 4 is smaller by a few inches and few ounces, and is used for kids from eight to twelve years of age. Size 3 is for under-eight year olds and tiny tots. The ball should always be inflated properly; overinflation could lead to injury. (See figure 1-3.)

It is essential for your child to own a ball. Any ball will do; there is no need to spend a lot of money. Practice is critical and can't be done without a ball. A local soccer club may buy them in bulk and give you a good deal on one. Owning a few balls is useful, even if they are used (try a garage sale). It saves a lot of time to have extra balls when practicing. I use a lighter volleyball for heading practice for younger kids. Little Hacky Sacks are also fun for juggling.

OTHER EQUIPMENT

The most important piece of equipment is a good pair of soccer shoes. Get a cheap ball if you must, but don't get cheap shoes. The ball control surfaces of the shoes should be smooth. Cleats are absolutely necessary for balance and changing direction quickly. Cleats cannot be pointy, and must be at least 1/2 inch wide and no more than 3/4 inch deep. I recommend high-top shoes, since sprained ankles are so common in soccer, but they are not necessary.

Shin guards are shields that protect the shin and lower leg. Most shin guards for youth players are made of fiberglass, but they can also be made of rubber or plastic. For some reason these are not required equipment, but they should be at all youth levels. When bones are broken, it's usually from getting kicked in the shin area. Shinguards are inexpensive, and are a must as far as I'm concerned.

BEGINNERS

Many coaches will be coaching first-time players, and perhaps coaching for the first time themselves. I was in this position myself many years ago. It was a bit intimidating, since I had never played soccer myself, and knew very little about the game. Yet, it was a wonderful experience, and the girls and I learned together. My lack of knowledge about soccer was really not a problem, since at very young ages the players have minimal skills and can only take in so much.

At the youngest ages (four to seven years old), the game is completely different. Your approach and expectations as a coach or a parent, particularly if you know the game well, must also be different. That is not to say that the skills, concepts, and drills later in this book are not to be applied. They must be. It's critical to start right away with all skills, and with on-going discussion of the concepts of the game. It never ceases to amaze me how much kids can learn if they are coached clearly and given opportunities to practice what they have learned. However, at these ages general improvement will come slowly, and so while coaches need to press on, their expectations must align with the realities of childhood. This means that patience, tolerance, and repetition must dominate the coaching approach. The key to coaching beginners is to let them play, reward hustle, praise everything, and keep them safe. Make sure they all wear their shin guards, because feet fly fast and furious.

I will refer in this book to the various levels of play: beginner, intermediate, and advanced. There are no hard and fast rules on the ages that distinguish a kid's level of play. It will often depend both on ability and prior years of play. Most soccer programs have an under-eight (U8) level, and many have an under-six (U6) program. These are all beginners.

By age eight or nine (U10), some of the kids are able to develop enough simple dribbling and passing skills, and even some one-on-one technique, so that the game begins to appear like real soccer. Some kids are able to comprehend soccer tactics and simple concepts of team play. Intermediate play starts here. This is a swing or transition age level, with many who are still beginners, a number who are now intermediate, and maybe a couple who are advanced. The better players will be asked to play on all-star or traveling teams to play other towns, and the rest will continue to play in local clinic or recreation leagues. Clubs will field *A* and *B* teams based on a child's ability. All-star teams, particularly at ten to twelve years of age, are quickly exposed to advanced play. Any kid in his first year, no matter what his age, will be at a beginner level for a while.

Let's review the differences in beginner soccer in more detail:

U6: FOR FOUR- OR FIVE-YEAR-OLD CHILDREN

These are the tiny tots of soccer, and their games present a true picture of kids at play. U.S. Soccer Laws of the Game now call for teams of only three to four players on the field and no goalie. Kids play on a small field of 25–30 yards maximum size, with goals 6 yards wide by 2 yards high. Local club rules will often play up to five or six players. The recommended ball is size 3. Games last for four eight-minute quarters. All fouls result in a direct kick, with no defending player allowed nearer than 4 feet from the ball. Referees must explain all infringements to the offending player. Improper throw-ins can be retaken once. Substitutions are unlimited and may be done at any stoppage of play. Each player shall play a minimum of 50 percent of the playing time, and matches may be co-ed.

To a four year old, soccer is about kicking a ball and running after it. That's it! That's pretty much the scope of their interest. Passing, positioning, and other skills take years to sink in. The modern rules that keep the teams and fields small more quickly

1-4. **SWARM SOCCER: THE BEEHIVE**

Eleven of the fourteen field players are bunched up in this under-ten game.

foster skills development and promote a broader understanding of the game. Kids also get many more touches (contacts) with the ball. These rules minimize the *swarm-style* soccer (chasing the ball madly in a pack, like a swarm of bees) that characterizes beginner play. The swarm descends on the ball, surrounding it with flailing legs, and suddenly the ball squirts out, quickly pursued by the swarm. Any goals scored are completely by accident.

Coaches seem to shriek endlessly at the kids to not bunch up, to hold a position, and to pass the ball, but it just doesn't happen. (See figure 1-4.) Certainly these concepts should be taught, but I encourage you to adjust your expectations and exhortations to the realities of this age level. Players will bunch up, and when they score goals, it will usually be quite accidental. This level has nothing to do with competition. Scores are not usually kept. It's all about chasing the ball, and they will have great fun doing it. Let them have it.

Practices for this age level should last no more than an hour. See chapter seven for more on practices, including a detailed practice plan. I urge you to spend some time "talking soccer." Have the glossary of this book with you and talk about some key terms. Talk about the field and the different parts of it. Do this for each practice and don't underestimate the value of their understanding the game's lingo. Don't talk for too long, maybe five minutes, since young children's attention spans are short. Just cover a few topics. You will also need to focus on form: how to kick with the different parts of the foot, how to dribble with the inside and outside of the foot, how to do a simple juggle, how to do a throw-in. Then have them practice these

13

fundamental skills. Finish with a scrimmage. Have two coaches play along, urging the kids to not bunch up and to pass.

U8: FOR SIX- OR SEVEN-YEAR-OLD CHILDREN

This is still very much a beginner level, and, for many, it will be their first year of play. U.S. Soccer Laws of the Game call for teams of four to five players, no goalie, to play on a small field of 30–35 yards maximum size, with goals 6 yards wide by 2 yards high. Many local rules will play up to seven players. The recommended ball is also size 3. Games last for four twelve-minute quarters. As with U6, all fouls result in a direct kick, with no defending player allowed nearer than 4 feet from the ball. Referees must explain all infringements to the offending player. Improper throw-ins can be retaken once. Substitutions are unlimited and may be done at any stoppage of play. Each player shall play a minimum of 50 percent of the playing time, and matches may be co-ed.

At six or seven years of age, players are still little children. The dribbling skills for some are getting a bit stronger, and they will begin to consider passing the ball. The smaller number of players, again, should foster some passing and break up the swarm-style play, but only minimally. Coaches can consider keeping one player back on defense, since there is no goalie, to have players consider positions. The game will still be a swarm, but with increasing moments of team play. Reward such play loudly, and make a fuss.

Practices need to continue to focus on basic skills such as dribbling, throw-ins, trapping, and juggling. Continue to spend time, perhaps during a break, talking about soccer terms and fundamental concepts. With repetition it will sink in. Encourage parents to work on dribbling and trapping with their child. More information about learning and teaching these skills can be found in the next few chapters.

CONFIDENCE

It is wonderful to watch a youngster develop, especially for a parent who has supported her child's growth in sports. The early visions of awkwardness and frustration are replaced by ones of smoothness, grace, and confidence.

Confidence is an important part of any sport, including soccer. Confidence and aggressiveness go hand in hand, and it's not easy to distinguish the two. One will invariably lead to the other. An aggressive player is not afraid to throw herself into the fray (fighting for the ball in an appropriate way, of course). This type of player develops more and more confidence about her ability to do various things with the ball. A player with confidence in his developing skills then becomes more aggressive due to those skills. Without either confidence or aggressiveness, a child will be timid with the ball and nervous when he is a part of the action, and therefore unable to make a good play. This will only discourage him further. Confidence brings on the aggressiveness needed to beat an opponent to the ball. It relaxes the body and controls nervousness. It frees a player to look around to see what's best to do. Confidence encourages the child to do something on his own, to try something new, and thus to improve individual ability.

Parents can be key to developing confidence. Play with your children one on one, or two on two so you can help with their development. Let the children win a few times to allow room for confidence to grow. Counter any criticism they might face on the field from the coach and other kids by telling them that, with practice, they will improve and by reminding them to be patient. A child may be content to just hang on, and that's okay too. Children who want to improve can become better soccer players with practice and parental support. Growth and improvement are natural byproducts of practice, but they will occur more quickly with the help of parents.

01

DRIBBLING AND JUGGLING 02

THAT SPECIAL TOUCH

The most important thing you can do as a coach or parent is to encourage players to spend time with the soccer ball. A comfortable relationship between the player and the ball is what soccer is all about. More important to a child's success with the game than size, speed, or innate athletic ability is oneness with the ball, the sense of touch that makes the player feel more comfortable and confident with the ball.

Physical ability helps (a lot), but there is no control over what a child was born with, beyond some conditioning. Nonetheless, you can teach soccer skills and ball control. These things alone, if practiced, will make a child good enough to contribute significantly to his team and feel good about himself.

Most youth soccer players begin by being prisoners of the ball. Their entire focus is on the ball itself. They are, in effect, trapped by the ball, not yet comfortable with it. It slows them down, makes them feel awkward. Sometimes, they just want to kick it away in frustration. The only cure to this is practice. Eventually, ball control becomes natural. As this happens, their focus will expand from the ball itself and open up to the field around them. With this comes confidence and the true enjoyment of the essence of soccer, team play. But until they know the ball, until they can move freely and gracefully with it and are able to focus only a portion of their concentration on the ball and the rest on the field of play, the ball is like a great weight around them.

My daughter did not have great speed, but she worked at her skills and became an excellent soccer player and won statewide honors. She played intelligently, but more importantly, she knew the ball and developed confidence in her ability to control it. The great news to coaches is that this can be learned, which means it can be taught.

17

KNOWING THE BALL

The key to soccer is ball control, particularly at the younger ages where game dynamics and team play are learned very slowly. A player who can move with the ball will be most valuable to the team. Ball skills are fundamental and essential. They include trapping (receiving passes), juggling, heading, faking, dribbling, passing, and shooting the ball. We will discuss each in detail. They *must* be practiced, either alone or, even better, with a parent or friend. Remember, as a parent or coach, you can give pointers and, just as important, encouragement.

Before we get to specific skills, let's talk a bit more about knowing or getting the *feel* of the ball. A young player must perceive the ball as if it were actually a part of her foot, or at least connected by an invisible string. For instance, the foot shouldn't really *strike* the ball when dribbling; it should simply nudge the ball along, much like a basketball player shoves the basketball while dribbling. The way to develop this perception is to have the ball around as much as possible, so a kid can use every opportunity to get the *feel* of the ball. (See figure 2-1 on page 19.) There is a time and place for everything, but some players keep a ball under their desk at home and roll it under their feet as they study in order to become more familiar with the *feel*. Continual contact with the ball is the key to developing skills.

Hundred Touches Drill: The technique is very simple; have the players put the ball on the ground, and fool around with it. The great thing is that a child doesn't need a lot of space, only a few square feet. The child should repeatedly touch the ball, alternating feet. Here are some things they can to with the ball: Roll it back and forth with the sole and side of each foot; jump over it; roll it around the outside perimeter of each foot; kick it back and forth between each foot; tap it on the top, alternating feet; push it forward with the sole of the foot, then quickly pull it back, then tap it to one side. Have the children try a variation of touches with each part of each foot to get to know how the ball feels against each part and how it reacts. Don't have them stand in one spot to do this, but tell them to move around a bit, even rotate around the ball. This exercise can be done in the yard, or even in the cellar on a rainy day. Have the players do this for about five minutes a day.

One idea is to have players keep a soccer ball in the family room and suggest that they fool with it while sitting or watching television. Don't encourage kicking or dribbling in the living room; they should gently roll the ball around, back and forth, faster and faster, and under each foot. They can make it a game or a challenge, such as

2-1. **KNOWING THE BALL**

A: Touch the ball with the bottom of each foot.

B: Jump with the ball between the ankles.

C: Roll ball up the back of the leg.

D: Kick it between the feet.

E: Roll it under and around the sides of the foot.

F: Just fooling around!

19

counting the number of times they can move the ball back and forth between their legs, or the number of times they can jump with the ball locked between the feet. Another drill they can do is to jump and touch the top of the ball with the bottom of one foot, alternating feet, trying to increase speed each time. The main idea here is to encourage constant touching, rolling, and shoving to develop a feel for the ball.

Over my years coaching soccer, I have met a number of foreign coaches—English, German, and South American. They all say the ability to move *around* the ball, and to feel its contours and reaction to touches and nudges, is critical to executing ball control skills. It's important, so it's the place to start.

THERE ARE NO LEFT FEET

Some of you familiar with basketball may appreciate the value of being able to dribble and shoot with both hands. Once you know an opponent can dribble with only one hand, and only in one direction, then you can cheat a bit to that side as you defend against him. However, a player with equal skills in both hands is much tougher to stop.

So it is with soccer, perhaps even more so. A player who must rely on one foot to dribble, shoot, pass, or trap the ball is only half as good. Unlike our hands, our feet are more accustomed to being used equally, so it's easier to get that other foot going. If a player is right-handed, she is probably right-footed, so have her work on using her left foot. For a left-foot dominant player, have her work on using her right foot. Coaches should stress using the other foot during practice, requiring players to do various drills with their nondominant foot. Parents can support this while their child practices in the backyard.

If a child has a problem developing the other foot, and just can't seem to focus on it, take the soccer shoe off the dominant foot and make the child wear a boot or go barefoot. Do this daily for fifteen minutes, and use of the other foot will come around.

DRIBBLING: THE HEART OF YOUTH SOCCER

Most coaches will tell you that soccer is a game of passing and that the team that can execute a series of passes will control the ball, penetrate to the goal area, and score. They will say that too much dribbling is to be discouraged, that the percentages are higher to stop a dribble than to intercept a good pass, and that a good pass can cover a lot of distance quickly. They are quite right, particularly at advanced-level play, but dribbling is still the most important individual youth skill, and is the most fun for a child. (See figure 2-2.)

The passing theory doesn't work well at the youngest age levels. It takes a long time before kids get the idea. Beginners don't move to open spaces to receive a pass; they often run up too close to their teammate to get a pass, and they don't return passes. A child *must* know how to dribble. Dribbling is also easier to learn. Passing skills, learning to spot an open teammate, and the ability to receive a pass come slowly. Good dribblers are the ones who will stand out in a game. Go watch any game at the younger ages. Those who can dribble do quite well.

Once at a soccer tournament in Canada, a young French Canadian girl put on a dribbling demonstration, the likes of which I've never seen. She could move anywhere at will. It was soccer at its best and beautiful to behold.

Obviously, there is a time to dribble. Defenders must dribble less because they need to get the ball away from the goal as soon as possible. Instruct players never to lose the ball dribbling in the defensive one-third of the field; the risk is too great. Forwards are usually the best dribblers because, near the opponent's goal, there may be no one to pass to. They are often on their own. Wing forwards must be able to dribble at full speed to advance the ball toward the opposing team's corner.

2-2. **DRIBBLING**

Dribbling is the heart of youth soccer.

Children taught to dribble will make rapid progress and will be able to contribute to the team and feel good about their play. This skill will be a catalyst for other skills as confidence grows. Plus, players who can dribble will be able to move the ball to a position from which they can execute a good pass (once their teammates learn to get into position to receive a pass). Counsel the children against hogging the ball. If any player consistently loses possession while dribbling, the coach must react to fix that. I had such a situation on my son's team with a young boy. He was our best dribbler, and often could get around a defender. However, he began to rely totally on the dribble and was not developing the ability to spot open teammates. We talked about it; he worked on it; I had to sit him down a few times to make the point, but he became a more complete player.

As I've mentioned before, at very young ages, the normal game strategy is *swarm-style* soccer with all the kids chasing after the ball. The kid who dribbles best will control the game. Gradually, coaches will be able to get kids to play position and quit the swarming. Until then, there is often no one to pass to. So teach your child to dribble.

TOP NINE FUNDAMENTALS OF DRIBBLING

1. Foot position. The player should use the instep, the area of the foot covered by the lower shoelaces, for straight-ahead dribbling, and the inside or outside of either foot to change direction. (See figure 2-3 on page 23.) Some players are more comfortable with the outside of the instep, with the foot slightly turned in or pigeon-toed for more control. A dribble starts with the foot closest to where the ball happens to be. The dribbler moves the ball softly by making contact about halfway up the ball with the foot. The knee is bent over the ball, so the movement is like the strut of a thoroughbred horse. The dribbler then switches the ball to the foot farthest away from the defender.

2. Eyes up. In dribbling, it's important for the player to keep his eyes up, not looking down at the ball. The dribbler needs to be able to shift focus from the ball to the field. The idea is to be able to see the field, the defenders, and the teammates. It's tough at first, but it comes with practice, with getting to know the ball. A coach needs to remind players regularly to "keep your eyes up." Remember, this is quite difficult at first, so be repetitious and positive. (See figure 2-4 on page 24.)

3. Sweep the ball. While dribbling, the player doesn't strike the ball; instead it's more of a gentle nudge or a sweeping motion. This relates to the concept of feeling the ball. Players learn to feel the ball through their shoes and control it. The ball becomes part

2-3. DRIBBLING FOOT POSITION

A: Use outside of foot to push ball to the outside.

B: Use instep to push straight ahead.

C: Use inside of foot to control and keep ball under body.

of the foot, and is carried down the field, or swept as if in front of a broom. (See figure 2-5 on page 24.) A useful gimmick to teach this concept during dribbling drills is to tell the players that they should not be able to hear the foot strike the ball. When the ball is kicked, there is a clear sound from the contact, since the foot and ball are together for only a split second. When the ball is shoved, or swept, the foot and ball are in contact for a much longer time, so there is no sound. The longer the foot is in contact with the ball the better a player can control it.

Longer, softer contact, or a sweeping motion, allows the dribbler to control both the speed and direction of the ball. Speed is important so that the ball moves at the same speed as the player and doesn't get out too far from the player where a defender can steal

23

2-4. **KEEP EYES UP**

Knee up, eyes up, legs are in a prancing movement.

2-5. **SWEEP THE BALL**

Sweep or shovel the ball out to the side

it. Directional control allows the dribbler to place the ball away from any nearby defender. Since the foot is in touch with the ball longer, it can better control the ball's speed and direction. Obviously, there are times when the dribbler will strike the ball, particularly when there is no defender nearby, and the best play is to kick the ball a greater distance and run up to it. However, the sweep is the primary dribbling concept. Other terms that can be used to convey this concept are *push the ball, drag it,* or *carry it.*

4. Under the shoulders. With a defender close by, the player must keep the ball in the space the width of his shoulders to protect it from the defender. This also allows the dribbler to fake and feint and to move the ball quickly in any direction. It's important to have all options open. In close quarters, the ball must stay under the shoulders. The dribbler may push it out and away for speed only when it is safe to do so.

5. Maintain body balance. The dribbler must be balanced with her weight evenly distributed, not leaning too far forward. Sudden changes of direction and the need to fake, feint, or change speeds all require a sense of strength and balance. The ball should be positioned, if possible, in the center of the body, so that the player is balanced and has the option to go in any direction. The player needs to always feel in control.

6. Move against the defender's direction. With the ball under the line of the player's shoulders, the player has many options. The ball can be passed, kicked back to a free teammate, or dribbled around the defender. The option chosen depends on many factors, including how the defender is sized up in terms of ability and speed. Most successful dribblers start with a move opposite to the defender's direction. The player must always know where the nearest defender is, and which way that defender is moving. Usually, the best play is simply to move the other way, catching the defender off balance. This means if the defender is approaching from the left, the dribble should go left, forcing the defender to change direction and be off balance. The technique is to sweep the ball past the defender, lift the ball high and wide enough to rise over an outstretched toe, then slide by the defender and go to the ball quickly before he can recoup. (See figure 2-6 on page 26.)

7. Fakes make space. Defenders won't make it easy for offensive players to dribble past them. A good defensive player will not commit too early, and will not charge the ball without believing it's possible to get a foot on the ball or a shoulder into the dribbler. Therefore, offensive players often need to make the defender commit to one direction, and then go the opposite way. This is done by *faking*. Faking is the art of making a defender believe that the dribbler is going to move in a certain direction, thus getting her to move in that direction as the dribbler goes the opposite way. The amount of fake needed depends on how savvy the defender is. Let's look at faking and feinting in more detail.

a) Head fake. Sometimes a head fake to one side is enough to get the defender off balance. The player tilts her head or upper body slightly to one direction. Tell your players that the defender must be made to believe the ball will move along a certain path, so the fake must be convincing. A key here is for the player to pretend to *pull* the defender a certain way. Players should make eye contact to help make the fake convincing, and then, with explosive quickness, go the other way. The fake only affords a split-second advantage, so it must be capitalized on. The defender will recover quickly.

b) Body fake. Usually an offensive player needs to make a whole body fake. This can be done by taking a full step in one direction, without the ball, and then moving with the other foot in the opposite direction while sweeping the ball with the outside of the foot. This fake works most effectively in a scissors move: the faking step sweeps the foot over the ball pretending to hit it, and land-

25

2-6. **MOVING AGAINST THE DEFENDER'S DIRECTION**

A: Defender approaches from the left.

B: Dribble to the left, against the defender's direction.

ing that foot to the opposite side of the ball. Then the ball is swept the opposite way with the outside of the other foot. (See figure 2-7.) Sometimes the offensive player needs to double fake (start and stop suddenly) nudging the ball and controlling it with the sides or bottom of the foot. The dribbler must determine the defender's balance, make him lean or commit to a direction, and explode the opposite way. The ability to control the ball, gained by countless hours of playing around and getting the feel of it, will allow a child to use the ball to control the defender as well.

c) Feinting. *Feinting* is similar to a fake, but is more of a hesitation or change of pace. A dribbler may pretend to slow down or simply change speeds. As with any

2-7. FULL-BODY FAKE

A. As defender approaches, dribbler begins to fake to her left.

B. She sweeps over ball with left foot further faking a move to her left.

C. She then sweeps ball to opposite direction with outside of right foot.

fake, feints throw defenders off balance and slow them down so that the offensive player can move quickly out. One effective feint is for a player to pretend to sweep the ball, then to stop short, letting the defender commit to a certain direction. Sometimes it's useful for a player to just hold the ball, gain time, and let the defender commit first.

8. Sweep out and explode to open space. If there is no defender nearby, or once the nearby defender has been faked out, the player's first move is to sweep the ball into open space and burst after it. This first move is critical. It's important to remember that an intensive, convincing fake must be followed by an explosive move the opposite way. This allows the player first to capitalize on the defender's being off balance, and then to run up to quickly advance the ball downfield or to have time to execute a solid pass. There may also be another defender upfield, so the dribbler needs to circle back into the open space and look for a pass receiver. Dribblers should usually flow away from the pressure. If there are no defenders in the open space, then the player can kick it further, in effect passing to himself and running up to the ball.

When faking or feinting, the player must remember that the defender, though off balance, will be able to stick out a toe in desperation. The dribbler needs to get the ball a few inches in the air, so that it sails over the defender's toe. Be sure to add this hint to drills that practice the body fake move.

If the fake and explosive thrust are successful, the player will have a second or two to decide what to do next. He can run with the ball toward open space if no defender is threatening and move the ball upfield a bit, or he can look for a teammate and execute a pass. The key is to get a moment to decide what's next. Ball skills can buy that time.

9. Shielding. Another helpful hint for a player being challenged by a defender is to keep her body between the ball and the defender as much as possible. This is called *shielding* or *screening* the ball. It can buy some time for a teammate to come up and help. If the player is running with the ball, screening obstructs the defender and makes it more difficult for him to get to the ball without fouling.

The player should place her whole body between the defender and the ball—side to the defender, knees bent, rump out to block. (See figure 2-8 on page 29.) A common mistake is to keep the ball between the legs. The player's body should be as low as possible, making it seem wider. This allows the dribbler to be ready to spring in any direction. The player must avoid turning her back to the defender; so

2–8. SCREENING

When playing ball, use shoulder, side, or rump to screen.

2–9. THE CHOP

Chop inside foot across front quadrant to stop or change direction.

as not to lose sight of him, she should keep a shoulder pointed at her at all times. Arms can be out to widen the screen, but should not be held too high. It's a good time to be aggressive; dribblers shouldn't be afraid to lean into the defender's body to keep him away. Here is where the foot rolls and ball touch come in handy to find a way out of the pressure.

TOP NINE DRIBBLING MOVES

1. The Chop. This move is a quick downward chop across the front quadrant of the ball with the inside front of the foot in order to stop the ball quickly. The foot is angled across the front of the ball to one side. The body hops a bit, turns perpendicular to the ball's direction, knee bent inward, chopping downward with the inside of the foot, just under the laces. The idea is to make a rapid transition to move the other way. (See figure 2-9.)

2. The Cut. This is a simple change of direction with the middle inside of the foot during a full dribble. The idea is not to stop the ball, as with a chop, but to change direction, usually to protect against an oncoming defender. As with dribbling itself, the player

29

should carry the ball, sweeping it to a position just in front of the other foot. It's good to get the sense of dragging it.

3. The Scissors. Described previously, this is a standard dribbling fake move. Make sure to keep the ball under the shoulders when faking contact with the outside of the faking foot, then plant that foot and sweep the ball the other way with the outside of the other foot. (See again figure 2-7 on page 27.)

4. Turns. Often a player will receive a pass with his back to the goal, and must, under pressure, find a way to turn and advance the ball. One simple technique is the *half-turn*, where the player receives the ball and makes slight contact with the outside of one foot, just enough to control the ball as he turns with it. Another way to execute a turn is for a player to stop the ball with his sole, and then quickly pull the foot back, advancing the ball in the same movement. If the ball is moving slowly, a player can step over the ball and then make contact with the outside of the same foot, diverting the ball's path.

5. The Check. Running at top speed, the dribbler suddenly plants one foot near the ball and then hops into the air, tapping the top of the ball to stop it dead with the sole of the other foot. This is a great play when a defender comes up from behind on one side. It buys time as the defender sails on by.

6. The Push-Pull-Tap. Under pressure, a player can execute a series of rolls with the sole of his foot on top of the ball, forward and back, side to side, or in a *V* pattern, followed by a tap out to open space. Often the tap will need some lift to get over the outstretched toe of the defender.

7. The Backdoor. A player runs up to the ball, his plant foot landing past the ball. The ball is swept behind the plant foot with the inside of the other foot.

8. The Swivel. Under pressure from one side, the dribbler swivels his hips to the side of the ball toward the defender, then sweeps the ball with the outside of his other foot away from trouble.

9. The Pirouette. A rarely seen, but interesting, move. A player runs up to the ball, stopping it with the sole of his foot and then jumps across the ball with the other foot, pirouetting with the first foot still atop the ball. He turns in mid air, and upon landing, now facing backward, pulls the ball back with the same sole, then spins again until he's facing forward, a full 360-degree turn in all.

DRIBBLING DRILLS

Several drills are great for improving dribbling skills. At beginner levels, the drills can be done without pressure, adding pressure as the players can take it. At advanced levels, the dribbling moves are all done one on one under simulated game conditions.

1. Quick Touch. This is the best drill there is for a beginner. Players stand in a small area and practice rapid sudden moves with the ball, using the inside, outside, and bottom of each foot. They touch the ball, roll it, make various sudden movements, and even dance with it. After a while, you can add some slight pressure by trying to take the ball away from the child, one on one.

2. Dribblemania. Like Quick Touch, but more structured, the dribbling moves on pages 29 and 30 should all be demonstrated and practiced, especially the first six (the Chop, the Cut, the Scissors, Turns, the Check, and the Push-Pull-Tap). They can be practiced anywhere and are good for parents, too. If you practice along with your children, you will learn the drills with them, so you can better relate to them. Do each one ten times, and then do combinations of them. After a while, apply some light pressure. For beginners, slowly go through the form and angle of the foot and knee. Do one at a time.

3. Sharks and Minnows. Mark off an area with cones and give each kid a ball (you'll need at least four players). One kid is the shark who tries to get the others' balls. Once a kid loses her ball to the shark, she grabs it and holds it over her head with legs outstretched. She may not dribble again until another player kicks a ball between her legs.

4. Slalom. A popular drill is to set up six to eight cones in a straight line and have a player dribble and weave through them, circling the last cone and returning to the start. Sometimes I had my daughter weave to the end cone and then speed dribble back in a straight line. I used to measure the time it took. Kids love racing against the clock. Begin by setting the cones five feet apart, and vary the distance from time to time. (See figure 2-10 on page 32.) If you don't have cones, use cups, plastic glasses, old milk containers, anything at all. You can vary the drill in innumerable ways. You can require each player to use only one foot or the insides or outsides of both feet. Several players can be on the course at one time to add to the need to be alert. Remind them to keep their eyes up.

5. Speed Dribble. I used to place a cone about 60 feet away and have the players dribble to the cone and return as fast as they could. Someone would time them and they were

2-10. **DRIBBLING AROUND OBJECTS**

Set up cones or plastic bottles 3-5 feet apart and have players dribble around them.

required to remember their personal best time, and try to improve upon it. The idea is to run *with* the ball, allowing it to roll only a few feet in front of the player. Don't let them just kick the ball 30 feet and run up to it. Tell the players to try to develop a rhythm, striking the ball with every other stride.

6. One on One. As skills improve, you can slowly begin to add some pressure. A good drill is to place two players (or you and your child) inside a square area about 20 feet by 20 feet (or smaller), then fight for ball control. If one person loses the ball outside the square, the other person gets control. This drill helps to teach screening, whereby the player learns to keep her body between the ball and the defender. You can also have plyers practice fakes and ball-touching skills. Make the area larger or smaller as needed, but attempt to make it progressively smaller as skills improve. Place two cones 3 feet apart for goals, at each end, and play a one-on-one game.

7. King of the Hill. This is one of my favorites, also called *knock out*. Place all players in a square area. Everybody has a ball. Each player must attack another ball while defending his own. Once a player's ball is knocked out of the square, that player is out. Disqualify any player who does not try to attack. It's fun, and it teaches dribbling, shielding, timing, and competition.

JUGGLING

Juggling is the art of controlling a soccer ball above the ground and tapping it up repeatedly with the foot or thigh (or even the head), not allowing it to touch the field. It teaches players how the various parts of their bodies may be used to control the ball. It is a great way to learn ball control, and is an essential drill for coaches and parents to use with their players. Juggling is probably the best confidence builder of all drills for the beginner.

Juggling benefits all ball-control skills: dribbling, trapping, and passing (particularly trapping). It also improves quickness with the ball and helps players develop the kind of feel for the ball discussed earlier.

When juggling, the player uses the same surfaces of the body that are used to receive and control the ball. These are the upper forehead, the upper leg and thigh, and the inside, outside, and top of the feet. One other surface, the chest, can be used to receive the ball, but is not very useful in juggling since it is difficult to bounce the ball up again. The tops of the shoulders are also available but are too bumpy for good ball control. The outside of the shoulder is part of the arm, and arms don't exist in soccer. If any part of the arm touches the ball, it is a foul.

Juggling is one of the first skills taught by most youth soccer coaches. It's not easy to learn, but it's fun. Players will struggle to get from two to four consecutive juggles, then on to five or six. But juggling increases by leaps and bounds. I've heard that some players can juggle for hours at a time. Juggling teaches young soccer players how the ball reacts to contact and how the surfaces of their bodies are used to control the ball, while making them alert to an errant bounce.

BEGINNING TO JUGGLE

One of my fondest soccer memories is the first week of practice with my daughter's team. We knew very little. I invited a few girls from the older team, and they put on a juggling show. The girls loved it, and tried to do a few themselves. A few years later they were showing off to even younger girls.

Just tell your players to try to keep bouncing the ball off their flat surfaces. Usually it's easiest to start with the upper legs and then move to the top of the foot. Encourage use of the forehead and the inside and outside of the foot as soon as possible. (See figure 2-11 on page 34.)

The key to juggling is to concentrate on the bottom center of the ball and to think about making the body surface as stiff and as flat as possible upon contact. Contact should be soft enough to control the ball. Players shouldn't hit the ball too high, just up a foot or two each time. Let them establish a rhythm. Have the players try to feel the ball under their shoes; not strike it, but try to catch and tap it, feeling the contact.

2-11. **JUGGLING**

A. Head juggling

B. Foot juggling

C. Thigh juggling

Players should count the number of times they juggle successively before the ball touches the ground. The idea is to try to do one better than their previous records. Encourage players to practice at home and reward improvement; make players want to be good jugglers.

Beginners Drill: A good beginning technique is for players to hold the ball between their hands and drop it onto the thigh, using the thigh to bounce the ball back into the hands. Then they should bounce it twice and do the same with the foot. Players can use the hands until they are no longer needed.

Intermediate Drills: Hhave players try to juggle with the foot. It's best to start on a hard surface as opposed to a field. Drop the ball to the ground and then, as it bounces, have them catch the bounce and tap the ball back to the hands. After a while, have them drop the ball directly to the foot for a tap back to the hands. Then let them tap it up, bounce, and tap it up again. Try to get the two-tap down solidly. At this point they are ready to try an actual juggle. Drop the ball to the foot and tap it up repeatedly with the foot. It will be very hard to get to three and four reps, and harder still to five or six. But once those first few taps are mastered, they will improve rapidly.

Remember to encourage your players always to do one better each day. Ask them to try to use all surfaces in a juggling sequence—foot, thigh, and forehead. And *you* should practice juggling too. It's awkward at first, but you will improve. Then, you and your players can practice team juggling.

TEAM JUGGLING

Two players can juggle one ball together, usually heading or kicking the ball back and forth. The player receives the pass, juggles to get control, and then passes the ball back. Sometimes, a child can juggle a ball off the side of the house or a wall; again the idea is simply to promote repetition. As in all sports, repetition and constant contact with the ball are the secrets to developing sound skills. When a child is in a tough game situation, the ability to use these skills will be critical to her success.

ADVANCED BALL-CONTROL MOVES

The following moves are for more advanced players. There is no specific age when it may be possible for kids to do these things. It depends on their skill level and desire to learn them. However, very young children and any beginner will certainly not be able to do these, and these are not essential soccer skills at the youth level.

Rainbow: A rare, but stunning move. This is a form of juggle where a player flips a ball from behind him over his head, so it lands in front of him. The dribbler plants one foot directly in front of the ball, touching it. The other foot, toe-down, reaches behind the ball and pulls it up the back of the plant leg, about calf-high. Then, that back foot comes off the ball and steps forward. The plant foot snaps the toe down and heel up, tapping the ball with the heel up over his head and landing in front of

35

2-12. **RAINBOW**

Step over ball with left foot and roll it up back of left leg with instep of right foot. Push off with left foot and lift it quickly, kicking the ball with back of left heel.

2-13. **BICYCLE**

With back to target, flip body back and kick airborne ball backward.

him. Some players can tap the ball with the sole of the foot, but it's much tougher to do. It's a nice show-off move. (See figure 2-12.)

Bicycle Kick: Another specialty move is the bicycle kick. With his back to the target, a player fields a ball in midair. He brings his non-kicking leg up to his chest, leaps up and backward, then brings his other leg up so that the movement looks like pedaling a bicycle. As the player falls back, he pedals his legs and kicks the ball while nearly upside down. This is often called a foul and dangerous play if a defender is very close because it could lead to injury. It should not be taught, but the kids often find a way to learn it at advanced-level play. (See figure 2-13.)

PASSING AND TRAPPING

03

In 1986, a team of sixteen-year-old German boys was hosted by soccer clubs in our area and played against some of our teams. One of the boys stayed at our home. When the Germans played our high school team, it seemed as though they had twenty-five players on the field. There was always a group of three or four players within passing distance, surrounding our players, and they were able to move the ball at will. We all learned a lot about the value of passing the ball. In 2006, our league hosted a similar visit. The local boys' high school team had a tie game going until the last two minutes. I was proud of how far American soccer had come just in my lifetime.

3–1. HAVE A CATCH

Great practice and a lot of fun for parents and kids.

After a few years of beginner soccer, in which dribbling is the dominant skill, passing becomes the primary and most important part of the game. The team that maintains possession will usually win, and a good pass to an open player helps to keep possession better than any other skill.

It takes two to pass, so encourage your players to pass with each other for a few minutes each day. They can go out into the yard, or find any space about 20 or 30 feet long, and pass to each other. (See figure 3-1 on page 37.) Encourage parents to pass with their child if other children are not around—it's a perfect parent-child drill. Kids can pass off a wall to themselves, moving around a bit. Tell them to think about pass location and ball speed.

Most passes are short to a nearby teammate, and these short passes maximize the chance to keep possession. Others are quite long, and can advance the ball far upfield. Passes can be made with the outside, inside, or instep of the foot. They can also be made with the head. Passes can be low to the ground, line drives, or chipped high into the air.

TOP TEN FUNDAMENTALS OF PASSING

1. Settle the ball. Many players get excited when approaching a moving ball and try to *one touch* it, or pass it right away without first trying to control or dribble the ball. It is much easier to use the first touch to get the ball under control and then try to pass it. Players should always first slow the ball down and get it in front of them and under control; otherwise the chance of executing a good pass is quite low. A bad pass often leads to lost possession. Of course, there are times to run up to the ball and one-touch it, particularly when under pressure or in front of the goal.

2. Use proper foot position. This foot is sideways, toe up, heel down, ankles locked, and knee over the ball. The foot is perpendicular to the ball, ready to strike about half way up the ball with the arch of the foot, just over halfway back, near the anklebone. The toe points up a bit, even with the heel, and the ankle locks and freezes. The foot should make contact with the ball at the lowest part of the sweep. (See figure 3-2 on page 39.)

3. Hop and plant. Particularly for a long instep pass, a player should approach the ball and plant the non-kicking foot up next to the ball, 5–6 inches away, pointed in the direction of the intended pass, so the toes are even with or just past the rear of the

3-2. **MALLET PASS**

The most typical and accurate short-range soccer pass.

3-3. **HOP AND PLANT**

A small hop as foot is planted provides a natural rhythm. Plant foot short and to the side of the ball.

ball and pointing at the target. If the plant foot is next to the ball, then the kicking foot will meet the ball at the lowest point in the kicking arc. Kids often plant the foot well behind the ball, but this lessens control and power. Planting the foot behind the ball should be done only when needed to lift the ball, causing the kicking foot to make contact on its upswing. Of course, lifting the ball is also accomplished by striking it a bit lower and leaning back some. A small hop just before the foot is planted produces a useful rhythm. Practice the hop and plant. Have the players get in the habit of observing where the plant foot lands. (See figure 3-3.)

4. Keep head down and look at point of contact with ball. Players often take their eyes off the ball just as they kick, lifting the head. Instead, they should not only look at the ball, but should focus their concentration on the very spot where they will kick it, right at the center of the rear bulge, halfway up the ball, at a point opposite to the direction they want it to go. Such concentration is particularly important if the ball is moving, and helps to avoid poor contact. The soccer ball, on a short pass, should move low to the ground, just a few inches above the grass. Have your players observe the height of the passes. Check the height of the ball. If it bounces, the contact was too

39

high; if it rises, the contact was too low. Once the pass is away, the player then looks up to see what the next move is.

5. Decide if contact should be with the inside, outside, or instep of the foot. The choice of foot surface depends on where the receiver is. As noted previously, most passes are short and use the middle inside of the foot.

The inside of the foot, anywhere between the heel and the big toe, produces the most accurate passes. It is also the best to use for one-touch passes since this area has the largest surface. However, it is less useful for powerful or long passes since twisting the leg prevents the full body power from getting involved. The inside pass technique requires lifting the leg, bending the knee, keeping the toe up, and then striking the ball in front of the anklebone. The kicking leg acts as a pendulum, swinging from the hip. Players should avoid the tendency to lean back since that will reduce power and follow-through.

The outside of the foot is used to shove or flick short passes. Contact is usually made with the side of the foot just at or below the smallest toe, usually in a flicking motion. This can be quite deceptive since it's a very quick pass, and the passer usually leans in the opposite direction, pulling the defender that way. Another deceptive pass is to kick the ball backwards with the heel. A player steps over the ball and kicks back to a trailing teammate.

The instep is used when power or distance is needed. Most passes are relatively short at young ages. Obviously, a long pass has a greater chance of being intercepted. However, crossing passes, passes far into the wing, clearing kicks in front of the goal, and corner kicks all usually require power and distance, and therefore differences in technique. The head needs to be lower, allowing more drive to the kicking foot. The plant foot will be further from the ball. (See figure 3-4 A on page 41.) The hips are more involved in generating power; the leg speed is faster, more powerful, and the kicking arc (the sweep of the foot) is larger. (See figure 3–4 B.) The body hinges at the waist, the upper half snapping forward, exploding from the belly. Ankles are rigid, toes down, and the player should snap and straighten the knee vigorously upon contact. It's helpful to curl the toes a bit, to help keep the toes down. The body leans back farther than normal to allow some lift to the ball. Passers strike with the instep, the lace area of the shoe, either directly on the large bone of the instep or just to the inside of it. Players with bigger feet will need to turn their ankle a bit. Have the players experiment with the ankle position that works best.

Finally, there is the chip shot. This is a short pass that travels high in the air, usually just over a defender. It's often used in free kicks. The player comes to the ball at

3-4. **INSTEP PASS**

A: Plant foot back a bit and stretch back for a long pass.

B: Curl the toes like a fist.

C: To chip the ball high, plant foot back and lean back, striking the ball low.

D: Knee over the ball, point toe down, and lock ankle.

an angle, planting the foot farther away from the side of the ball than normal, leans backwards to fully extend the kicking leg, and lifts the ball. Keeping his head down, the player should strike the ball low, in a chopping motion, with the front inside of the foot, but not follow through. (See figure 3-4 C.)

6. Kick with leg speed. Many kids get into the habit of kicking with a lazy foot, but the idea is to snap the foot into the ball with speed.

7. Follow through. Players don't really strike at the ball as much as they kick *through* it, so the foot follows through its sweep in a smooth, full arc. A long follow-through should pull the body forward, requiring the planted foot to hop a step. This is called a *push pass* because the long follow-through seems to be pushing the ball.

8. Know where your teammates are. A key to successfully passing a soccer ball is always knowing where the nearest teammates are. The best passers are able to *see* the playing field and know who is free.

This is not as simple as it sounds, and involves much mental discipline. At U6 and U8 levels, there are only a few other teammates on the field, so kids can learn to keep an eye out for them. At older levels, there are seven to ten field players, depending on the age group, and it becomes more difficult to see the whole field. However, the player needs to concentrate mainly on those who are around him, particularly just ahead of him and to the side. The closest players should always be kept in mind because most situations require a pass to occur very quickly in order to take advantage of an opportunity or protect the ball from a nearby defender. Therefore, players need to focus only on two or three teammates. The remaining teammates are farther away, and for most youngsters are likely out of range.

Downfield players need to let players in front of them know where they are. As will be discussed in chapter six, communication on the field is the heart of both offensive and defensive strategy. It's helpful for parents to remind their children, if the referee allows such coaching, to "know who is around you." Call it out from time to time to help your child develop the habit. It just takes a split second to pick up the location of teammates. The time to do it is when the ball begins to approach. It encourages the child to begin to think about what to do if the ball is passed to him.

9. Pass in front of the receiver. The most common mistake in passing is passing the ball behind the receiver, forcing the play to slow down or stop. The error occurs when players pass directly at other moving players, and not in front of them. It's necessary to judge a player's speed, and get the ball to where that player *will* be.

Another common error is passing too hard. This may make it difficult for another player to receive or trap the ball, or the ball may miss the receiver entirely. If the pass is too soft, it allows a defender time to intercept. Discuss these concepts with your players. Passes should be firm with enough speed to get to the receiver ahead of any defender, but not so hard as to roll past him to the defender.

A player needs to know the wind when passing, particularly if the wind is strong. It's usually a good practice to keep passes low, to minimize wind interference. The wind can be a friend or a foe, and much of this depends on using it. In order to use it, a player needs to know which way it is blowing and how strong it is. Many passes are pushed out of bounds by a strong wind.

10. Keep moving. Players should keep running down the field after a pass. A player is not a spectator; there is no need for him to stand and watch his pass. Passers must keep moving immediately. They can move to the ball if the pass or reception was bad, move for a give-and-go, or move to open space, whatever is appropriate for the situation.

PASSING DRILLS

1. Name and pass. Players form a circle and pass the ball to each other. Receiving players must call out the name of someone in the circle before receiving the pass and then, touching the ball only once, pass it to that person. That person, in turn, must call another name before the ball arrives and pass it one-touch to that player. It is difficult, but it teaches players to look up at the field and pick out a receiver before they get to a loose ball.

2. Triangle drill. Set up some 15-foot grids with cones and position players near three of the four cones. Have them pass to a teammate and then run to the free cone. Do some one-touch and some two-touch pass.

3. Foot position. To drill long passes, have beginners take their socks off and demonstrate to them the position of the foot for different types of passes. Show them the large bone of the foot for longer instep passes and, with the shoe on, have them kick the ball out of their hands with the instep to get the feel for the foot position. (See figure 3-4 D on page 41.) When first teaching the instep drive, players may stub their toe due to improper knee angle. It's useful to practice kicking off a small paper cup to get the proper form, then cut the cup in half, and eventually eliminate it.

4. Scrimmages. Small scrimmages of three to five players each also teach passing dynamics, particularly if the players are limited to two touches each, one to trap and one to pass. This forces players to know ahead of time which players are available for a pass. A one-touch requirement makes the drill even harder. Set up a few cones or plastic glasses a few feet apart for goals. Play in the scrimmage with your players. These small-sided games are great fun and great practice.

RECEIVING OR TRAPPING

A good reception begins with a good pass. The idea is to place the ball one to two yards in front of a running receiver. Too often, the pass is behind the receiver, forcing the player to break stride to control the ball. The delay gives a defender more time to attack, so the receiver must work much harder. The terms *trapping* or *receiving* are often used alternatively. Trapping is used primarily, but I like the term receiving, since that's what we want to do.

Receiving skills are best developed by juggling the ball, as described in chapter two. Juggling teaches the player how to use the flat body surfaces, forehead, chest, thigh, and the sides and top of the foot to control the ball. Receiving a pass requires these same body surfaces. However, there are some differences requiring additional skills.

First of all, the ball often is moving laterally, so the receiving body surface needs to be turned out to receive the ball. With individual juggling, the ball moves up and down; team juggling allows for lateral movement of the ball.

Second, the ball is moving quickly, often very quickly. When it contacts the flat body surface it can bounce far away. Many times in youth soccer, you will see a young player receive a pass and watch as the ball bounces 20 feet away. To avoid this, the player must learn how to soften, cushion, or deaden the surface by retracting as the ball makes contact.

Third, players want to control reception in such a way as to lay the ball down in front of them, ready for the next play. A player may wish to receive and pass with a single action. As mentioned earlier, this is called a one-touch pass.

TEN BASICS OF TRAPPING

The best way for a child to learn to receive passes is to become a good juggler. The next best way is to practice receiving passes, and this is something that is done best with two players, or a parent and a child. So let's talk about a few basics.

1. Get to the ball. Often the pass will not be exactly to the player's foot. She will need to run to the ball. Often it's just a loose or deflected ball. The nearest players must then engage in a foot race to the ball. Winning teams are the ones that win most of these races. It's not just a matter of speed; it involves hustle, courage, and a strong determination to get the ball first. I can't emphasize enough the importance of this. *You* can't emphasize it enough to your players. There are times on a soccer field when a player must run as fast as possible, not as many times as you might think, though, because body control and the need to maintain balance often requires the players to slow down a bit. However, when there is a loose ball or a pass, the idea is to go 100 percent to get to the ball, and then aggressively claim it. Players must believe they can win all balls for which they have a 50-50 chance. (See figure 3-5.)

As a parent you can be helpful. Talk to your child about the importance of being aggressive when going to the ball. Don't be too critical when she gets beaten, but talk to her, especially if she is not trying hard enough. The Showdown drill at the end of this chapter is excellent for developing aggressiveness. It also helps players to anticipate when they will get beaten, and thus to slow down and assume a defensive posture. All of this needs to be done quickly, but the quickest thing is just to get to the ball.

2. Play the field conditions. If the field is dry, the ball will bounce higher; if it is wet, it will tend to skip. Of course, players have to be aware of how the ball may be hooking or slicing, how the wind is blowing, and where other players are. There is time to look for defenders and teammates as a player runs to the ball; although, as noted earlier, a player always wants to know where nearby teammates are. The angle and speed of the ball also need to be judged, and the final decision is which body surface to use to catch the ball, depending on the height of the ball, or the height of its bounce.

3–5. GET TO THE BALL

The moment of truth: Soccer games are won and lost depending on which team gets to the most loose balls, one on one.

3. Meet the ball. Sound the same as getting to the ball? Not really. Often a ball will come right at a player, but he still needs to move toward it, particularly if a defender is approaching. How often do we see a child stand and wait for the ball, just to have another player fly by and scoop it away?

4. Take command of the ball. Often, in youth soccer, a high pass is allowed to bounce. Understandably, children prefer to field the ball low, with their feet. They are less confident with their upper surfaces and are a bit timid about heading or chesting the ball. Unfortunately for the player trying to receive the pass, bounces must go up and come down again, giving time to a defender to apply pressure. Also, bounces can be unpredictable, especially if the playing surface is not smooth. The idea is to use the head, chest, thigh, or even foot to stop the ball in flight and get control of it quickly so that a player can pass or dribble without hesitation.

5. Face the ball and present the body surface. At the right time, when contact with the ball can be made in a controlled manner, a player should face the ball and present the body surface. The body weight should be balanced or on the non-receiving foot. A flat surface will control the ball; the inside or bottom edge of the foot will usually give the most control. The word *trap* actually derives from the notion that a good way to receive a pass is to trap the ball under the foot. This is done by turning the foot sideways, toes pointing out and up in the same manner as in a push pass, but with the foot elevated about 4–5 inches above the ground so it can trap the ball under the foot. This trap can also be done with the outside of the foot, toes turned inward and down, body turned a bit away from the ball. The ball is caught and cradled along the outside of the foot.

The instep, head, or chest are used mainly for receiving high-lofting passes. A player catches these high balls with the instep as they drop close to the ground (if there is time). When a player uses the chest, he must keep his balance, with his knees bent, body arched, and arms out, keeping his eyes on the ball. He shouldn't arch his back too far too soon or there will not be room to absorb the ball. (See figure 3-6 on page 47.)

6. Relax at the point of contact. The moment of contact between the ball and the body surface requires undivided attention, balance, and concentration. A player must focus on the point of the ball where contact will be made and think about what direction it then should take. The idea is to relax at the moment of contact. "Hurry up, then wait" is a useful coaching phrase. Too often kids will hurry the trap, get excited, and boot it away. Players must take enough time to trap well.

3-6. **TRAPPING: PRESENT THE BODY SURFACE**

A: Present the upper thigh; keep balanced.

B: Present the forehead, relax on contact.

C: Present chest, lean back, but leave room to lean back further upon contact.

7. Deaden the surface or withdraw. Receiving a soccer ball is no different than a baseball or a basketball. In these sports, the player learns to keep the hands soft, otherwise the ball will bounce out. It's no different, and even more important, with soccer. Think of the difference when a ball hits something hard, and when it hits something soft. Players want the body surface to be soft. Another word you can use to get the idea across is to *deaden* the surface. Describe it as letting the foot feel a bit limp.

At the point of contact, the player actually *catches* or cushions the ball by slightly withdrawing the surface away from the ball to make it even softer. This should result in the ball dropping gently to the ground, guided to a point just in front of the other foot, which is ready to dribble or pass. If receiving the ball with a part of the body other than the foot, present the surface and then slightly withdraw it. (See figure 3-7.)

3-7. DEADEN OR WITHDRAW SURFACE

A: Present the receiving surface; deaden the ankle.

B: Withdraw to further soften the moment of contact.

8. Decide where to place the ball. As skills improve, the ball can be dropped in different directions depending on how close defenders are and where the player wants to go. The trick here is first to know where to drop it, and then carry the ball to that spot by angling the body surface as it traps the ball. Most often players will want to drop the ball in front of them, close to the free foot, so this should be practiced the most.

9. Volley. Whether heading the ball or receiving it with the foot, the option exists to simultaneously strike the ball in midair to another player or into the goal. This is called a volley. Here the surface is not withdrawn, but actually strikes or rebounds the ball, often quite a distance. This move involves a fair amount of skill. Players are usually instructed, and should usually try, to first catch the ball, get control, and then execute the next move. However, there is a time for everything and the volley skill should be developed. The volley is used most after a shot at the goal or, defensively, to clear a ball in front of the goal. (See figure 3-8 on page 49.)

10. Now get going again. The last part of every move is to get going again. Receiving the pass is only one part of a fluid action. Once the player has controlled the ball in front of him, he must execute the next move, whether it is a dribble or a pass. Players should be constantly in motion, especially when near the ball.

Eyes on ball, point plant foot at target and come around quickly with instep. Lean as much as needed to get full extension on kick.

TRAPPING DRILLS

I have mentioned a few passing and receiving drills in the prior chapter already. Here are a few more.

1. Wall Kicking. After juggling, this is perhaps the best drill there is for both passing and trapping skills. Find a wall—the side of a store, or a high cellar foundation—for kids to practice kicking against. You can easily build your own: Lean a piece of thick plywood against a tree, or build a frame on the ground. If you do this, dig a small trench to sink it a few inches into the ground for more support. Concrete walls are best because they give a good hard rebound. The rest is easy: Have the players kick the ball and trap the rebound. Pick out spots on the wall and have the players try to hit them, then move up closer to practice receiving. Remind them to use the instep, inside, and outside of each foot. Practice placing the ball at different spots on the ground after it is received. Have them try some one-touch action, and then go for controlled traps and passes.

If the wall is tilted back a bit, it will rebound the ball in the air. This will allow practice receiving with the higher body surfaces such as head or chest. Two people can do this, and you can make a game of it, scoring points for missed traps by the other person.

2. Two-Person Drill. There is no substitute for practice with another player. You can go out yourself and work with your child for twenty to thirty minutes. If you do so regularly your skills will improve, too. Get about 25 feet apart and kick the ball back and forth. After a while you will be able to add motion to the practice. A great two-person drill is to run down a field passing the ball back and forth. Try to lead each other with the pass just enough so the player doesn't have to break stride. My daughter and I used to do another drill where we would stand about 2 feet apart and just tap the ball back and forth quickly. We used to count to see how many we could get before one of us messed up.

3. Keep Away. I mentioned earlier the one- or two-touch passing drills. Divide players into two teams of two or three players each inside a square area. Count the number of consecutive successful passes, and the team with the most wins. If the ball goes outside the square due to a bad pass or a missed trap, the ball is awarded to the other team. This drill obviously is as good for receiving as it is for passing.

4. Showdown. The best drill for aggressiveness in trapping and in getting to the ball is to have two players stand about 30 feet apart. Throw the ball between them. As soon as it touches the ground they charge it. Make sure the ball rolls a bit so they are not coming directly at each other on a collision course. A variation is to have them stand near each other, and then throw the ball away from them, letting them run to it after it touches the ground. Again, this is a drill a parent and child can do together. As a coach or parent, you can control the drill, allowing the child to get a few balls to build confidence.

SET PLAYS AND SPECIALTY SKILLS

04

THROW-INS

When the ball is kicked out of bounds along the sideline, the team responsible for kicking it out loses possession. The referee need not touch the ball, but will merely point in the offensive direction of the team being awarded the ball. The ball is thrown back in from the spot where it went out of bounds, usually by a halfback or fullback. The general idea is to throw the ball to an open player, wherever that person might be. It's preferable of course to throw upfield, optimally into the wing area near the sideline, to a teammate.

The reasons to throw upfield along the sideline are twofold: First, it advances the ball in the direction of the other goal; second, the receiver can use the sideline to shield the ball, thus eliminating one direction from which a defender may attack. That being said, players shouldn't throw the ball in to a player in heavy coverage just because he's along the sideline; the best option is to find an open target.

Usually the wing forward (a forward playing to the left or right side of the field near the sideline) will stand facing the thrower and either receive a pass with the feet or break upfield to receive a longer throw. Another good play is to throw to the foot of a teammate who can simply one-touch pass it back to the thrower. A third option is for the wing to break toward the thrower, creating space in the area vacated, while the center halfback breaks toward the vacated wing area for the throw. Similarly, a fourth option is for the receiver to start to run upfield, then quickly come back to receive a short pass. (See figure 4-1 on page 52.)

THROW-IN FORM

The proper form for throwing a ball into play from the sideline has several specific regulations:

4-1. THROW-IN PLAYS

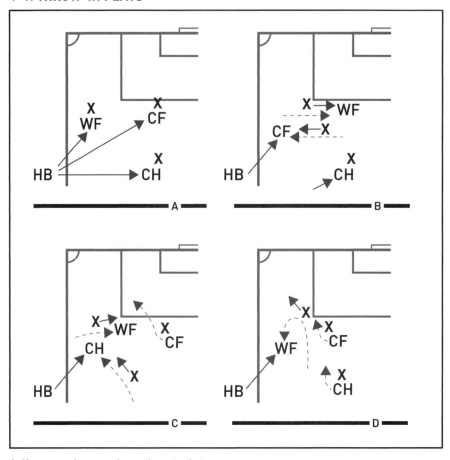

A: If someone is open, always throw to that person.

B: Wing forward creates open space, going to middle; center forward switchesto wing area for throw.

C: Wing forward vacates, creating space, center halfback moves up for throw.

D: Wing forward runs upfield, but quickly comes back for throw.

1. The ball must be thrown with both hands evenly in one continuous motion.
2. It must be delivered from behind and over the head.
3. It must be thrown straight in front of the head, without twisting off to one side.
4. The hands must follow through without the ball; it can't be just dropped to the ground.

5. Both feet must be touching the ground as the ball is released.

6. The ball must land on the playing field, otherwise it is thrown again.

7. It must touch another player before the thrower may touch it again.

The most common violation is a raised back foot as the body leans forward into the throw. The penalty for violating any of these rules is loss of possession. It's surprising how often violations occur for this relatively simple play. Upon violation, the opposing team gets to throw the ball in from the same spot. (See figure 4-2 on page 54.) As noted in chapter one, at U6 or U8 levels the child will be given a second chance on an errant throw-in.

KEYS TO THROW-INS

1. Quickness. The nearest person to the ball when it goes out of bounds should scurry after it, or look for the ball-boy, and quickly throw it in before the defense gets organized and *covers*, or marks, potential receivers. Offensive players need to make their move at the moment the player throwing in raises the ball overhead, possibly before the defense can react.

2. Accuracy. A good throw-in gets the ball directly to a teammate's foot, in the air or on one bounce. If the space in front of the teammate is open, then the player should throw the ball ahead and let the player run up to it.

3. Distance. Another key to throw-ins is strength and the ability to whip the upperbody to get distance and speed on the ball. The thrower holds the sides of the ball with the fingers spread apart behind the ball in a *W* shape. She then brings the ball back behind the head, elbows pointing outward. Feet should be shoulder-width apart, one foot in front of the other. The player then bends back her upper torso and snaps forward with the ball, releasing it with the added momentum. I've seen kids who can throw nearly to the goal, setting up nice scoring opportunities.

If a player can throw only a short distance, there is much less that can be done. Practice is important. Have your players throw to each other, and over time, slowly add distance between them. Have a contest to see who can throw the farthest. I used to have my teams practice throwing a basketball since it weighs more. I've heard of a medicine ball being used as well. The idea is to arch the back and whip the ball, using the legs, back, and arms. The throw-in can be done with the feet together, one in front of the other, or stepping forward, as well. Stepping forward generates more power but also leads to lifting the foot. The standing throw avoids this problem.

4-2. **THROW-INS**

A: Throw with both hands evenly, from behind and over head.

B: Throw to foot of a teammate.

C: The most common mistake is to lift the back foot.

D: Throw with both hands evenly from over-head, not to the side.

4. Drag the back toe. Lifting the back foot is the cause of many penalties. It's a natural tendency to lift the foot as the ball is thrown. On a running throw the body's forward movement tends to pull the foot up, and players should practice dragging the back toe to keep it down.

5. Re-enter to open space. Finally, after the throw, the thrower should quickly get back on the field of play and move into position to receive a pass back from the target or do whatever is indicated by the circumstances.

THROW-IN DRILLS

1. Form drill. Have players line up along the sideline and throw the ball in while the coaches watch their form. Common errors coaches should be on the lookout to correct include using one hand more than the other to add power, throwing downward instead of forward, lifting the back foot, and holding the ball to one side rather than directly overhead.

2. Distance throws. Have players line up and see how far they can throw. Let them measure (approximately) their best throw, and try to beat it the next time. See who can throw the farthest and use them whenever possible during games.

3. Accuracy throws. Have players stand 15–30 feet away and practice throwing to their feet. Eventually add a defender to pressure the trap.

CORNER KICKS

The corner kick is a free kick from the corner near the opponent's goal, with a whole group of teammates on the spot. This is an ideal scoring opportunity, and goals are often scored this way. Corner kicks are allowed at all levels of play.

Corner kicks are awarded when the ball goes out of bounds crossing the goal line, not the sideline, and a defensive player touched it last. The referee will point toward the corner of the field indicating a corner kick will be taken. A player, usually the wing forward, will place the ball at the corner of the field and kick it, trying to land it directly in front of the goal. The corner kicker may not kick the ball forward and receive it himself. At younger ages, the kid with the strongest instep drive will often take all corner and free kicks.

The typical tactic for corner kicks is to line up a wall of teammates outside of the penalty area and have them charge the goal as the ball is kicked. The players then attempt

04

to score. The more advanced ones usually try heading the incoming ball into the net. I like to see the majority of players involved in the penalty area: six or seven players on a team of nine to eleven; five out of seven or eight players; or four if the team has five or six players. (See figure 4-3.)

A common strategy for playing a corner kick is to have the three tallest players charge the goal from just outside of the penalty box near the far post and angle toward the goal looking to head or kick the ball in. I instruct players to switch positions and cut in front of each other as they charge to the goal in order to confuse defensive players who are trying to mark a specific offensive player. The offside rule is in effect as soon as a player touches the ball, so the players must be mindful of where the ball is.

4-3. CORNER KICKS

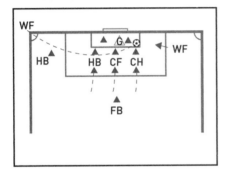

A: Halfback (HB) up for possible short pass, wing forward (WF) on the other side if ball gets through, three players crash in from the 18-yard line for a shot.

B: Approach ball with a power move, plant and full stretch back.

C: Hinge forward from waist for power and follow through.

If you have more than three players available for a corner play, have one head toward the far post at the opposite wing in order to retrieve the ball if it passes the goal untouched, one angle toward the corner kicker for a possible short pass, and another player or two remain outside the penalty-area line to get the ball if it squirts out. Someone must stay at midfield in case an opponent breaks away with the ball toward your goal.

As mentioned, youth teams often will have a big player who can kick the farthest come up and take the corner kick. If the ball drops in front of the goal, the chances to score are greatly increased. See the section on "Passing" in chapter three for the proper kicking technique. As I have already mentioned, the object is to *power kick* the ball, and the kicking technique is 1) for the right-footed kicker, lean a bit to the left of the ball to allow more kicking foot extension; 2) reach back farther with the kicking foot; 3) curl toes and lock ankles firmly; 4) explode into the ball with foot speed; and 5) follow through. (See figure 4-3).

If the wind is strong into the goal, the kicker should aim the ball in front of the crossbar, and attempt to score *with the kick*. It happens more than you might think. Otherwise, the idea is for the ball to meet a teammate about 6 yards in front of the goal at head height.

At young ages, a teammate can quickly run toward the corner kicker and receive a short pass. That player can then center the ball to the front of the goal, or give it back to the corner kicker for a center pass. Again, they must watch for offside. It occurs often on corner kicks. After kicking, the corner kicker usually should head toward midfield. He is too far away to help offensively, and needs to get back onside anyway. He can help best to cover defensively at this point.

Defending corner or direct kicks will be covered in chapter six.

FREE KICKS

As reviewed in the discussion on rules in chapter one, upon a foul the referee will award a free kick, a direct kick if the foul was intentional, and an indirect kick otherwise. Your players should understand the differences and look for the referee's signal. For a direct kick the referee will point to the goal, and for an indirect kick he will raise his hand (see Referee Signals on page 141).

It is usually advantageous to take the direct kick immediately, before the defense forms a wall. (We'll discuss walls in chapter six.) If there is a scoring opportunity, have your strongest kicker take the shot, and try to lift the ball over the wall or curl it around the edge of the wall. Have another player or two try to stand in the wall of defenders, and then move to create an opening upon the kick. These players can also trail the ball, looking for an opportunity to score.

On an indirect kick close to the goal, two players must touch the ball. One approach is to have a teammate gently tap the ball to the shooter, who then takes a direct kick to the goal in an attempt to score. The shooter must kick the ball immediately since the defense will charge at the first touch. Another approach is to loft a ball to another player charging toward goal for a header shot.

A penalty kick is a direct kick awarded to the offense when a defensive player commits a foul in the penalty area. The kick is a free shot on the goal with nothing obstructing him but the goalie. Everyone else must leave the penalty box. Such kicks are not generally allowed below U10 level of play. Usually, the player who was fouled takes the shot. The ball is placed on the penalty spot, and the shooter takes a few steps and kicks the ball. The goalie cannot move until the shooter's foot strikes the ball. The shooter should aim to hit the ball just inside one of the goalposts.

Another free kick is the goal kick, taken by a defensive player when the offense kicks the ball out of bounds past the goal line. A goal kick is generally kicked from the corner of the goal area. Usually, a fullback will kick the ball and the goalie covers the net, although a goalie with a strong foot will sometimes take the kick. (See figure 4-4.)

4–4. GOAL KICK

Taken from the corner of the goalie area, a strong foot is most valuable to get the ball far from the net.

HEADING

Heading is usually one of the last skills learned by children. They do not practice heading for obvious reasons. It can hurt, giving a slight headache or sore neck if improperly done. However, there is a way to avoid this problem.

At intermediate levels, soccer balls come in two main sizes, 4 and 5. Size 4 is generally used by players under twelve years old. Size 3 is used by players under eight years old, but they won't be heading just yet. Instead, I recommend getting and using the smaller ball (size 3) for heading practice for players up to twelve years old, and size 4 thereafter. It sometimes helps to let a *little* air (not too much) out of the ball to soften it up a bit. I've used volleyballs for heading practice since they are much lighter than soccer balls. Toss the ball lightly to your players to build strength and confidence. A good drill is to have the players kneel down to practice so they learn not to jump or lunge at the ball.

The key points to emphasize to players about heading are:

1. Concentrate.
2. The hips are square to face the ball (power comes from the hips).
3. Lean back a bit, keeping eyes open (mouth closed to avoid injury to teeth and the tongue).
4. Both feet should be on the ground in a boxer stance (one foot out, one back) and the body balanced.
5. Look right at the point of the ball where contact will be made.
6. Make the neck rigid.
7. Make contact with the middle to upper forehead.

Sometimes it is necessary to leave the ground in order to get high enough to head the ball on its side when another player is also trying to head it. Players should avoid lunging at the ball, but instead jump straight up. Often kids will cringe, close their eyes, and let the ball land on top of the head. That's not only terrible mechanics, providing no control of where the ball goes, but it also hurts. The upper forehead just below the curve is the strongest part of the head. Using this part of the head allows for continued eye contact and control and placement of the ball. The player should try to make contact with the middle of the ball's bulge, at a point in line with where they want it to go—just as with kicking. Talk about the point of contact when practicing headers. It's critical to focus on a point on the ball. Contact above the center of the ball will drive it down, contact below mid-center will drive it upward.

59

The player must know what to do with the ball before it arrives. Then it's just a matter of execution. One option is to retract the head, trap the ball, and drop it to the ground for ground play. This is all right if defenders are not too close. The second option is to pass it with the header. This requires a decision of where to strike the ball to send it in the right direction, and how hard to strike it to get the desired distance. By simply turning the head a bit, the player can change the direction the ball will go. Practice, practice, practice is needed to do this effectively. The head and shoulders alone are used for short passes. For longer passes, the legs should be used to give strength and distance to the headed ball. This technique is for a player to get under the ball with his legs in a boxer position, arch his back, tense his upper body, draw in his chin, and then thrust his head through the ball. He can't just let the ball hit the head; he must take command of it. (See figure 4-5.)

Heading is often done in front of the goal in an attempt to score or to defend. Many goals are scored by heading. Players should try to head the ball very hard, and aim downward to make the goalie's job more difficult.

Heading is also used against punts and goal kicks when the ball is high in the air. Since the ball travels a long distance before it is headed, it has the greatest potential

4-5. **HEADING**

Eyes on ball, neck rigid, body balanced, in a boxer position.

to hurt. This is an advanced skill. I strongly recommend that beginners not undertake to head such balls, and do not teach heading long balls at all to U10. After that, when they have had sufficient experience and practice, and the neck is more muscularly developed, it can start. Coaches may urge kids to do it, but if you are not sure your child is strong enough, tell him to forget it. You will each know when to undertake heading very long balls, probably not much until U12 or later.

HEADING DRILLS

1. Start slowly by having a player hold the ball near the head, toss it up a few inches, and head it back to the hands. Slowly add height to the tosses. After a while, have players try to head the ball to a teammate. I once saw a coach hang a ball from the goalpost in a nylon stocking to demonstrate heading practice.

2. Pair up players, initially 8–10 feet apart and add distance over time. Have one player toss the ball up toward her partner's head, so she can head it back to the tosser. Have each player do it five times, then switch. After a while, players should try to head the ball back and forth. At a more advanced level, use three players.

3. Have the pair of players practice tossing and heading from a seated, kneeling, squatting, and leaping position. Have players do it five times, then switch. (See figure 4-6 on page 62.)

4. Have players toss or loft the ball from the wing area, crossing in front of the goal to a teammate who tries to head it into goal.

TACKLING

This skill can be risky business. By definition, a *tackle* is an attempt to remove the ball from another player. In chapter six we teach that defense should usually be passive, either falling back or slowing down the ball. The primary principle of defense is never to let the ball be dribbled past you. In tackling, this chance is taken. If the player fails, the ball gets past her and the offense gets a higher percentage attack because the tackler is now out of the play. There are times when tackling has a better chance, such as when the dribbler goes down the sideline and can be hemmed in, when a player is double teamed, or when another defender is covering the area.

There are a few types of tackles. One is the *block tackle*, which involves blocking a forward dribble with the side of the foot and endeavoring to lift the ball over the

4-6. HEADING DRILLS

A: Start slowly, just tossing lightly to the head.   **B:** Practice on the knees to learn to avoid lunging.

dribbler's foot and behind him, or kicking away the ball when it gets too far out in front of the dribbler. This is a safe and effective way to steal the ball. It's basically a timing play, picking the moment when the ball is far enough away from the dribbler to be taken away. (See figure 4–7 A on page 63)

Another tackle is a *standing bump* or a *shoulder tackle* by which the tackler steps in between the dribbler and the ball, usually approaching from the side, and bumps him with the shoulder. (See figure 4-7 B.) The tackler steps in between with the plant foot and takes the ball with the outside foot. The bump should not be too aggressive, more a leaning in with the shoulder than a push.

Timing is important. It's good to feint a tackle and then charge when the ball is dribbled out. Another good time to tackle is just as the player receives the ball and does not yet have it under control. Shoulder contact is permissible, but the player must keep the arms in and not shove. The shoulder is used to stop forward progress, and the inside of the foot is planted firmly in front of the ball.

Finally, there is the *slide tackle*. Generally, I view it as an advanced skill and do not encourage it unless the player has command of the skill. Even then, the tackle is used only when an opponent has beaten a player to the ball and there is no other chance to catch her but a tackle. A slide tackle is a dangerous desperation play. It's dangerous

4-7. TACKLING

A: Block tackle. Block from the side, hit the ball first.

B: Shoulder/hip tackle. Defender in white steps in with right foot and hip to take control.

because missing the ball may lead to a penalty. Also, the tackler is now on the ground, clearly out of the play, even if successful. Like everything else, there is a time for it, especially when a forward is going at the goal and the tackle is the only hope.

The technique for a slide tackle is similar to the slide in baseball. One leg is tucked in for cushion, hands raised to avoid injury. Players should not slide from directly behind the opponent or a free kick and red penalty card will quickly be called. They must come in from the side. If a player touches the opponent before the ball, a foul will be called, and quite possibly a caution card.

SHOOTING

Every team needs someone who wants to score, who thinks about it constantly. Beyond desire, shot accuracy is the most important talent. It comes from shooting the ball thousands of times from all angles. Juggling and passing drills are very helpful, but shooting the ball under pressure, with a goalie attempting to block the shot, is the best practice. If your child is a forward, get a goalie and defender (you, another parent, a sibling, or friend), and let the child shoot repeatedly.

The upper corners of the net are the best targets; the lower corners are the next best. Players should aim for the far goalpost, because shots across the goal are harder for the goalie to stop, and they leave a chance for another player to intercept and shoot the ball if the first shot is wide. Ground shots are usually tough for the goalie to catch.

Shooters kicking from a distance need to get power from the instep. They should curl the toes and lock the ankle so the foot is like a fist, snap the knee as striking the ball, and hit the middle of the ball. Players need to see the point on the ball they will strike, and hit through that point. They must keep the weight forward, chest and knee over the ball, and plant foot astride the ball or else the shot will sail high over the crossbar. As with any hard pass, the head must stay down and still. It's important to ensure that the plant foot is not too close to the ball, which reduces power, nor too far behind the ball, causing too much loft.

Usually there is little time to settle the ball before a shot, so a one-touch volley is needed to contact the ball while it is still airborne. Instead of trapping a ball that is a foot or two off the ground, the player one-touches it directly at the goal. With the leg raised, knee bent, and lower leg pointed outward in the same plane as the incoming ball, the player strikes the ball with the instep. These skills must be practiced. Concentration on the point of contact—dead center on the side of the ball—is needed. Players should take the ball out of the air or on a hop with the intention of putting it in the net.

Forward Drill: A parent or coach stands at the side of the penalty area and serves centering passes to a forward. Throw at first, and then serve by kicking centering passes. Even if there are just the two of you, it's good practice. You don't need a net, just a wall of some kind will do. Vary the speed, height, and location of the pass. Players should try to score one-touch goals.

FIELD POSITIONS

05

In youth soccer, anywhere from six to eleven players on each team take the field, depending on the age level. Even fewer players may take positions in the beginner clinics. Various formations can be employed, and these will be discussed in the next chapter. Different positions sometimes have different names depending on the league, club, or even coach's preference.

The players who play up forward, attacking the other team's goal and trying to score, are called just that, *forwards*. Fowards on the sides of the field can be called *wing forwards*. If they generally play on the right side, they are *right forward*, or *right wing*. It is the same for the left side, and left-footed players are a great bonus at the left wing position. The forward player in the middle of the field is the *center forward*. If there are two inside forwards (no center forward), then the one to the left is called the *inside left forward*, playing just inside the left wing. It is the same for the *inside right forward*. Forwards can also be called *strikers*, although I've often heard this term reserved for the center forward. (See figure 5-1 on page 66.)

The players who play back by their own goal, defending it, are called *backs* or *fullbacks*. On the right side is the *right fullback*, and on the left is the *left fullback*. These fullbacks are sometimes called *wing backs*. The one in the center is called the *center fullback* or *stopper*. Sometimes there is another defensive player who is even farther back than the center fullback and is called the *sweeper*.

A third group of players is halfway between the forwards and the backs, and they are called, not surprisingly, *halfbacks*, and sometimes *midfielders*. There are *right* and *left* (or *wing) halfbacks*, and *center halfbacks*. If there are four halfbacks, the two in the middle are *inside left* or *inside right halfbacks*.

Last, but certainly not least, not by a long shot, is the *goalie*, also known as the *keeper* or *goalkeeper*.

There are some guidelines coaches use initially to determine where players should be positioned. Parents can also use these to guide their children initially,

5-1. SOCCER FIELD AREAS

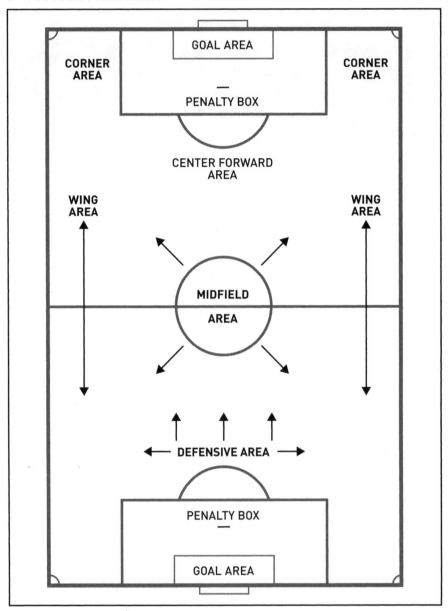

Forwards generally cover the forward half of the field, near the opponent's goal. Fullbacks are responsible for the defensive area, protecting their goal. Halfbacks play the midfield between the two penalty boxes. Wing players cover their assigned side. Of course, these areas are reversed from the point of view of the opponent.

although it's preferable to prepare your children to play multiple positions in their first few years. A rule of thumb is that the wing forwards have speed and the ability to dribble with speed. The center forward has speed, good skills, aggressiveness, and an innate desire to score. Halfbacks are endurance runners and usually have the best passing and trapping skills. The center halfback also needs leadership and game savvy. The fullbacks are big and strong, good headers, defensive-minded players. The stopper is aggressive and fearless. The goalie is often a superb overall athlete, with excellent hands, preferably tall with long arms, and much courage. Left-footed people play on the left side, or at least those with the strongest left feet. Vice versa on the right side. Those who play up the middle need to be able to use both feet effectively.

That's a good initial description of what's needed at each position, and your child will fit one of these categories. The nice thing about soccer is that it accommodates all sizes, speeds, and abilities. However, the bottom line is what happens on the field, and that is where positions are earned.

We'll talk a lot more in chapter six about the strategy and field dynamics relating to these positions. Initially, it's important that children understand the areas of the field they are responsible for, and not just roam all over the field chasing the ball. Eventually they will learn that they may leave their area under certain circumstances. However, forwards generally stay in the front half, fullbacks in the back half; left side positions stay left of the middle of the field, and right side positions stay on the right of the middle. Halfbacks play between the penalty areas.

We'll review field formations in chapter six. For eleven-player teams, the formation most in vogue is the 4-4-2, that is, four fullbacks, four midfielders, and two forwards. Even for seven-on-seven games, the formations use all three types: forwards, halfbacks, and backs, but in varying groupings, for example, keeper plus 2-2-2, or 3-2-1. Even a four-on-four game plays a diamond 1-2-1, with a fullback (sweeper), two midfielders, and a forward.

FORWARDS

Forwards are offensive players. Their main job is to score or to assist in scoring. As stated earlier, they must have speed to be able to break away from defenders and execute a strike on the goal. Forwards must be able to dribble. I remember a young girl with great speed. I played her at wing at pre-high school levels, but her high school coach moved her to fullback. He wanted her speed on defense. She was frustrated with the position and seemed bottled up. She needed to play up front where she could run freely. Eventually, she quit the team, although she could have been a great player if the coach had positioned her properly.

WING FORWARDS

The primary scoring strategy is for the wing forward on either side to dribble the ball down the sideline and get as close to the goal line as possible. Then he *centers* the ball, that is, passes it toward the front of the goal, to the striker for a shot. The reason teams need to attack from the wing is that the forwards on offense generally cannot advance farther than the ball. (See the offside rule in chapter one for more detail.) This rule essentially means that offensive progress needs to be *earned with the ball*, that is, offensive players cannot be further upfield than the ball unless there is a defender between them and the goal. The purpose of the rule is to prevent players from just hanging out in front of the other team's goal. Specifically, it states that a player without the ball can't be further forward than the ball, when it is played, unless the goalie and another defender are between him and the goal. So if the wing forward moves the ball up toward the corner, other forwards and the striker can also advance, keeping even with the ball, to the front of the goal area.

Another reason forwards strike from the corner is that it's much easier to advance the ball along the sideline than up the middle where defenders are more numerous and can approach from any angle. This means that wing forwards need two strong skills. First, they need to be able to *speed dribble*, to outrun a defending fullback into the corner of the field. Second, while on a dead run, they need to be able to execute a *centering pass* to the middle for the striker. While all basic skills are needed, speed dribbling and the center pass on the run are essential. I had a girl once with good speed who could get the ball into the corner, but she could not execute the center pass. Both skills are needed. (See figure 5-2 on page 69.)

For players in this position, these two skills should be practiced above all others. A speed-dribbling drill was mentioned in chapter two; have the forwards finish the drill with a centering pass each time. The trick is for them to plant the inside foot and, with a slight twist toward the middle, quickly come around with the passing foot and strike the side of the ball with the instep above the big toe. Repetition is the key; have them do it a dozen times each practice. A wing forward should start with the ball at midfield, speed dribble down the sideline, and then pass the ball to the front of the goal. You can run down the middle, as if you were a center forward, to provide a moving target.

68

5-2. **CENTERING PASS**

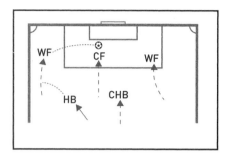

A: Ball is passed up to the wing forward who then advances it to the corner and centers it to a center forward for the shot. The technique is: plant foot points to center, quick kicking action, and hips open to goal.

B: Centering pass to a center forward crashing upon the goal area.

You can also practice defending against a child to provide some pressure. Young wing forwards need to learn how to fake and feint, stop on a dime or speed up, and give themselves a window for the centering pass. Not much is needed, only a split second and enough space to get the ball past the defender.

Wing forwards are sprinters; they should condition themselves with many wind sprints, about 30 yards each. It's essential to properly stretch before doing wind sprints. Also, encourage the child to develop the left foot. Any child who can execute a left-footed center pass will receive more playing time because most kids tend to develop only the right foot. Left-footed players should also work on using the right foot.

Wing forwards score plenty of goals. When breaking toward the corner they often can get away from the defender and strike directly at the goal. They can shoot the ball from their wing position if in scoring range. I always tell them to aim for the far goalpost because if a far-post shot is wide, there is still a chance for another forward to recover it. Wing forwards also head goals on corner kicks and jump on loose balls shot from the opposite wing. As a wing forward, your child should be encouraged to practice shots from the corner of the penalty area.

Wing forwards should generally stay as wide, or as close to, the sideline as they can. They shouldn't get caught bunching into the middle of the field. It's the halfback's job to get the ball up and out to the wing for an attack down the sidelines. If the ball is passed up to the wing corner, the wing had better be there to get it. Often the pass will be a long or cross kick—kicking across the field to a free team-mate—into the wing corner. The wing forward needs to be in position to sprint to

69

the ball, advance it, and execute the centering pass. That's why speed is necessary; it becomes a foot race.

Wings need to practice corner kicks and heading goals. They don't do throw-ins that often, since they are usually the players receiving them. Wing forwards should practice receiving throw-ins; this is something a parent can help with. Throw the ball to your child a dozen or so times from as far away as you can. Mix up the throws. Your child needs to learn to control many bad throws as well.

CENTER FORWARD OR STRIKER

The center forward, or striker, has speed, ball-control skills, and aggressiveness. Some height would be nice for heading, but the essential ingredient is a knack for scoring. In every group of kids, there is always at least one who really wants to score. Sure, all kids like to score, but I'm talking about the one who is always looking to put the ball into the net and who can get it there. The desire is essential. How often do you see players with the ball in front of the goal, and they don't shoot? The center forward must be constantly thinking of scoring. The player who produces goals will get to shoot; it's as simple as that.

The center forward needs to develop shooting skills, so this is what she should spend most of her time practicing. Stand your center forward on the 18-yard line (front line of the penalty area), marking the penalty area to receive passes endlessly from both sides of the field. Have someone stand in the goal so the child can get used to shooting around the goalie. Young players also need to practice scoring with just one touch. (See figure 5-3.) In a game there is often no time to settle the ball; have the striker focus on the point of contact and shoot, shoot, shoot. Get her to practice with each foot.

5-3. THE CENTER FORWARD

Lob passes to the striker for one-touch volley shots.

A center forward needs to be good in one-on-one situations, since this is what she is constantly faced with. Practice here will pay off in goals. The best strikers can score on a breakaway, and such situations must also be practiced.

A good drill is to put five or six forwards in the penalty area and keep throwing balls into their midst. The kid who gets the ball, shoots. Everyone else is to prevent the person with the ball from shooting. As soon as a shot is taken, throw in another ball. The winner is the one with the most goals.

FULLBACKS

Fullbacks are defensive players. Their job is to stop goals. When a goal is scored, it's not the goalie's fault. It's usually the defense's fault. The soccer goal is pretty big; fullbacks must stop players from getting close enough to take good shots.

WING FULLBACKS

Wing fullbacks on the right and left side have the primary job of containing the wing forwards. As I said earlier, the wing's job is to penetrate to the corners and center the ball. The wing fullback's job is to slow that penetration and stop the center pass. Fullbacks must stay between the ball and the goal, move with the fakes and feints, and look for an opportunity to get a foot on the ball. If they take a risk and miss, the chance for a score radically increases. They must be cautious, conservative, and alert.

We'll talk in depth about defensive strategy in chapter six. The key is to hold ground. Most kids make the mistake of overcharging the ball. An offensive player with even minimum skills will see this and simply sweep the ball around a charging defender. There are times to attack, especially if the player has backup, and there are techniques to help tackle the ball. More times than not, though, a charge will fail. When it does, the offensive player will penetrate and the charging defensive player is out of the action. So the idea is to hold ground, prevent or delay penetration, keep the dribbler wide along the sideline, wait for help, and seek good percentage opportunities to tackle the ball. (See figure 5-4 on page 72.) But remember, when a forward penetrates behind the fullback, no one is left but the goalie, and that's trouble. Talk to your players about this concept.

A fullback must know the location of any forward in the area and anticipate that the other team will try to play the ball to the wing. Good anticipation will often be rewarded with a stolen ball. When a halfback with the ball glances at the wing forward, odds are a pass will follow. The fullback anticipates this and breaks to a point between them to intercept the pass, or breaks into the corner to intercept a long pass.

5-4. **PLAYING FULLBACK**

One of the most important concepts in soccer is to hold ground, delay the ball, force or pressure mistakes, and above all don't over commit.

Wing fullbacks need to be able to do throw-ins if the ball goes out of bounds near them, and should practice them.

When the ball is on the other side of the field, the wing fullback must protect the area in front of the goal. He anticipates the center pass, and makes sure the center fullback covers the center forward, or he covers the center forward himself if the center forward is left unmarked. He looks for other forwards trying to sneak around behind the defense. Defenders mark opposing players in their zone. All players in front of the goal must be marked one on one by a defender.

CENTER FULLBACK

Most modern, eleven-player formations play four fullbacks. The two inside fullbacks can play next to each other, as inside left or inside right fullbacks, or they may play vertically, with the one center fullback, also called a *stopper*, up a bit and the other center fullback, the *sweeper*, behind him. Most often, the latter is used. At the younger ages, with less than eleven players on a field, three fullbacks at most are used. In a three-fullback lineup, if the center fullback plays a bit forward of his two wing fullbacks, he can be called a stopper. If he plays a bit behind the other two fullbacks, he can be called a sweeper. Usually, however, the term center fullback is used.

Other than the sweeper, the center fullback is the last line of defense. Center fullbacks must never let the ball get behind them. They must always know which players are in front of the goal and must mark, or defend, these players closely. They do not leave the area unless another defender is there to back them up. Communication is constant and essential. They must listen for instructions from the goalie, who has a broader field of vision.

Once a fullback has the ball, he tries to move it safely up the field. The center fullback must *never, never, never* pass the ball toward the front of his own goal. This is the cardinal rule of defense. Defenders must pass upfield, toward the sideline. If the area in front of them is open, they may dribble forward as far as possible. Other players will fill in the area behind them.

The center fullbacks are usually tough kids. They need to be very aggressive and absolutely determined to keep the ball away from the goal. When the ball is in the penalty area, they *must* get to it, and if under pressure, kick it away as far as possible. They must be willing to make a last ditch slide tackle. They rarely dribble the ball or take any chances in front of the goal. Their job is to get the ball away from the goal. They should endeavor to pass it safely to a halfback or even back to the goalie. The highest priority is to clear it away. The center fullbacks' best weapon is often a powerful clear kick, which sends the ball a long distance in any direction.

The center fullback must be able to head the ball away from the goal. He must take on any offensive player and beat that person to the ball without fouling or obstructing. If he does, particularly in the penalty area, the price can be very high—a penalty kick and most likely a goal.

As a defensive quarterback, the center fullback always looks for the offside and can call offside traps (discussed in chapter six on page 100). If the goalie gets caught out of the goal area or falls down, it is the center fullback who must go to the goal and try to deflect any shots, without using the hands.

SWEEPER

Usually teams utilize the sweeper position in an eleven-player formation. The sweeper usually plays behind the three fullbacks, but is often allowed to freely roam the defensive third of the field. Sometimes the sweeper is used to mark the other team's center forward one on one, or mark another gifted scorer. The primary mission of the sweeper is to pick up unmarked players near the penalty box.

HALFBACKS

As mentioned earlier, halfbacks are also called *midfielders*. Another name for them used primarily in England is *linkmen*. Halfbacks don't need size or great speed, but they are usually the most skilled and consistent players on the team. The center of the field sees the most action; that's where the ball is most often. The ball comes from every possible direction and height. When halfbacks have the ball, defenders come to them from all angles. They must be able to control the ball under great pressure. They are the long distance runners of soccer and are nearly always running.

My experience is that soccer games are won and lost at midfield. If the halfbacks cannot control the ball, it will wind up back by their fullbacks. The team that can keep the ball in front of the other team's goal the longest time will score. It's a game of percentages. Therefore, it's the job of midfielders to prevent the ball from penetrating through to their defense. They must control it and move it up to their offense. This is what wins soccer games.

WING HALFBACKS

Halfbacks don't need speed. It's good to have, but not essential. Their job is to control and pass the ball. They also need quickness—quick footwork, fakes, feints, whatever it takes to control the ball and advance it to a forward.

A typical routine for a halfback is to receive a pass from a defender, shield the ball, make a move, and get enough time to pass the ball forward. This is called the *transition*, where they start by facing their own defense, receive a pass, and turn to play the ball up to their offense.

A nice transition move for halfbacks receiving a pass from a fullback is called the *half-turn*. I learned it from some visiting British coaches. Facing the backfield, the player wants to receive the pass without slowing the ball down too much, turn and pivot with the ball under control, and advance it upfield. The idea is to trap the ball while turning on the other foot. The foot receiving the ball touches it only gently, slowing it down just enough to have it under proper control, and then guides it out in front of the player, to advance upfield.

Halfbacks do most of the throw-ins. This is because the forwards need to be free to receive the pass, and the fullbacks need to defend if the pass is intercepted. Halfbacks, more than anyone else, need to practice this skill. An effective throw-in is a valuable offensive weapon, particularly when near the offensive goal. There it can be similar in value to a corner kick.

CENTER HALFBACKS

The center halfback is the team's quarterback, the leader, often the most skilled player on the team, and the one who directs the offense by constantly calling out plays and directions. This player has the ability to see the whole field. The center of the field is where the ball usually is; it crosses this area all game long. The center halfback must control it, and get it up to one of the wings. The center halfback is also often a second striker, tracking the forwards and picking up loose balls and rebounds for shots on goal. This position requires the ability to shoot from a distance.

My daughter played this position, and she had an uncanny ability to see the open players and pass the ball perfectly to their feet. This is what midfielders must be able to do.

The center halfback helps out the wing halfbacks when they are in trouble, calling for them to *square*, or pass, the ball laterally to her. She then initiates the offense, generally dribbling if possible, then getting the ball up to one of the forwards. A key play for all players, and particularly the center halfback, is the *give and go* (discussed in chapter six). Usually, a halfback will give the ball to the center halfback who will quickly return it to the same halfback, who is then sprinting upfield. This also works with the center forward, who dishes it back to the center halfback and then moves into a forward gap.

The center halfback needs to be able to head the ball, so heading skills should be practiced. These players also receive many throw-ins and should work with the wing halfbacks on different routines.

GOALIE

Last but certainly not least is the goalie, or goalkeeper. The goalie must be a top athlete. In European soccer play, the goalie is usually the best athlete on the team. This player doesn't need great foot skills, but does need to be super quick, have excellent hands, be smart, courageous, able to punt a long distance, and be very, very tough.

At very young ages, certainly U10 or younger, goalies should not be locked into the position. Each team should have at least two or three goalies, and should try to give some experience at that position to all players, at least in practice games. Also, goalies should all have some playing time on the field in each game, and be involved in learning all offensive and defensive skills. The focus for coaching the youngster should be on stance, catching skills, throwing, and punting. The main issue for the children will be their nerves, particularly when they catch a shot or have a goal scored upon them. In the first instance tell the child to stay calm, take a breath, see the field around him, and then decide to run forward and throw or punt the ball to a teammate. As to goals, you must emphasize to the whole team that responsibility for a goal is rarely the goalie's fault, and is generally the result of a poor defensive play leading to an open shot. This is the case, and the team and the goalie need to know it.

TOP ELEVEN GOALIE FUNDAMENTALS

1. Stance. The goalie stance is a crouched position, with the hands down and out to the sides ready to block a shot to the side, weight forward on the front of the feet, eyes on the ball, ready to spring sideways into the path of the shot. (See figure 5-5.) It's important for the goalie to watch the ball in flight and follow it with his eyes right into the hands. The hands are close together when catching a shot, with fingers spread apart and thumbs touching in a figure *W*.

If at all possible, the goalie should use the body to back up the hands by getting in front of the ball. If the shot is low, the legs should be together. To stop a hard, direct shot, the goalie can hop back a step to cushion the ball, watch the ball all the way to the stomach, and pull it in.

2. Positioning. The goalie positions himself between the ball and the center of the goal, on an arc extending from the goalposts out a couple of yards from the goal line, never *in* the goal or standing on the goal line. Yet the goalie doesn't want to be so far out from the goal line that a high shot can get over his hands and still go under the crossbar. When the ball is in the opponent's half of the field, the goalie should stay up by the 18-yard penalty line, or even farther if he is fast enough. Sometimes a long pass from an opponent will go farther than expected, and the goalie can easily get to the ball first. This should be done only in rare instances, because one mistake and the opponent will have an open net. It happened once to me as I played goalie in a pick-up game. It was a most frustrating feeling to watch as the ball was easily taken to the net, well out of my reach.

5–5. GOALIE POSITIONING

The Goalie Stance: Crouched, weight forward, hands faced out protecting the sides.

5-6. DIVE: GIVE BOTH HANDS EQUAL PLAY

With body horizontal, both hands can be involved.

As players advance onto the goalie's side of the field, the goalie slides back, always on a line between the ball and the center of the goal. Naturally, in the thick of action, the goalie is less than 5 or 6 feet from the goal line.

3. Diving. For shots to the side of the keeper, goalies must hurl themselves laterally toward the ball, in a horizontal position. The concept behind the horizontal position is that it allows both hands equal play, since relative to the body they are centered. If the player merely reaches to the side, the hands are not equally balanced. Soccer balls are shot very hard, and both hands are needed to catch the ball. Horizontal dives allow both hands to be equally and comfortably engaged in catching the ball. (See figure 5-6.) The toughest job for a goalie is to dive on a loose ball because it can be scary when other players are also running toward it. I've always believed, particularly at youth levels, where the kids swarm in front of the goal, that goalies should have forearm guards and hard hats. Referees are usually pretty quick to stop play if a goalie is in danger. Still, too often, a player will try to kick the ball out of a goalie's hands, and this leads to injuries.

I used to lay a mattress out on the field for my son, and he would dive for the ball, landing on the mattress. After a while I put a small mat, and eventually he knew how to fall. Another good drill was to let him sit on the ground and I would throw the ball to either side of him. After a while he could kneel, then squat when receiving throws. By starting low, a player hits the ground much more softly and learns how to break the fall with the hip, and the upper arm and shoulder. He shouldn't break the fall with the hands or elbows because they break more easily.

4. Using the body. Ground shots are the toughest for a goalie to block. She must try to get behind the ball, legs only a few inches apart, knees straight, and scoop

5-7. HIGH SHOTS ON GOAL

Always catch the ball if at all possible, but punch or tip it over the crossbar if needed on a very hard shot.

the ball up with the hands close together, palms out. Another approach is a moving scoop whereby the goalie, with legs still close together, lowers one knee to a few inches above the ground, scoops up the ball, and rises quickly to move forward to throw or punt it to a teammate. Whether a ground shot or a shot in the air, it is always helpful to catch the ball using the body as a backstop, and backing up with the hands if possible.

5. Catching or deflecting high shots. Goalies also need to know how to time high shots. In youth soccer, many goals are scored on shots that go over the goalie's head. Your local high school may have a soccer wall with the goalpost area painted on it. These large wooden walls are often used for shooting practice. I made a lot of use of ours for goalie practice with my son. It's good for two people because the ball comes right back to you, and it saves a great deal of time. I kicked high shots, so he could begin to judge his timing of when to jump for the ball and to know how far out of the net he could safely come.

For any hard shots high enough to require the arms to be fully stretched upward, the goalie should learn how to tip the ball above the crossbar. (See figure 5-7.) It gives the other team a corner kick, but it's better than a goal.

A hard shot is tough to catch with outstretched hands. The goalie needs to learn what she can catch and what needs to be deflected. She should always catch a ball if possible, but tip it if needed. Goalies can punch the ball if it's necessary, particularly if in a crowd and it's tough to get both hands on it. A goalie can also kick a ball, but catching is by far the preferable action. A good catching drill for goalies is to throw a small medicine ball back and forth. This also strengthens the hands and wrists.

6. Charging on a breakaway. Occasionally, an opponent will break away from the full-back and come upon the goalie one on one. If this happens, and if there is no chance for a fullback to intervene, then the goalie must charge the opponent. He shouldn't charge too soon, allowing the opponent to loft a soft shot over his head, or pass to a teammate. As soon as the ball enters the penalty area, the charge is on. The goalie charges, arms outstretched, legs balanced, eyes on the ball and on the opponent's legs, anticipating the contact with the ball. Sometimes the forward will dribble the ball too far out in front and the goalie will be able to dive on it (dangerous) or tackle it (safer). The goalie must try to time the dribbles and charge as the ball is swept forward, particularly if it is dribbled out too far from the attacker. (See figure 5-8.)

In any event, the idea behind charging is to put pressure on the striker, obstruct the player's vision of the goal, and force an early shot. As the goalie charges, the available shooting lanes and angles become narrower, and it's much tougher to score. Often the shot will be wide, or deflect off the goalie. It's essential for the goalie to stay on her feet and be able to react to the loose ball. Once a goalie makes a charge, she must commit to it and follow through. Stopping halfway allows for a more open shot, or a dribble around the goalie, and can lead to a goal.

5–8. CHARGING THE STRIKER

A: Only when no other defender can assist, the goalie charges, hands out trying to force a wide shot.

B: Stay balanced, arms out, make the body wide when tackling the ball, anticipate the shot.

7. Looking for unmarked players. One of the goalie's main jobs is to look for opponents who have no defender marking them. The goalie identifies the player, usually by number, calling for defenders to mark the player. The goalie should not be afraid to shout to other teammates about what's going on; she has the best view of the whole area.

8. Calling for shots. On a long high shot—usually on direct or corner kicks—if the goalie can get to the ball she will shout out, "Keeper!" This instructs her teammates to get out of the way and let the goalie catch the ball. She should not say, "I've got it," since that is considered confusing. When the goalie cannot get the ball, she shouts, "Away!" as a signal that she is too far away and others will need to help.

9. Commanding the penalty area. The goalie must always know who is in the penalty area. The main offensive strategy is to get a centering pass in front of the goal, and strikers then look to head the ball into the net. The goalie must anticipate this, and snatch the ball away or block the headshot. It's often hard to judge when to run out to catch a high pass and when to stay and defend the shot. With practice, the goalie will know what he can do and what he can expect out of his defense. A good rule of thumb is that if the ball is in the goal box, the goalie should get to it; if outside of the goalie area, she should be cautious. However, it's always easier to catch a high pass than to defend a hard shot, so tell your goalie to get the ball whenever possible.

10. Making the decision to punt or throw. The goalie needs to be able to punt and throw as accurately as possible for both short and long distances. The throw involves curling the ball in the hand and slinging it underhand in bowling fashion, sidearm, or overhead, as needed for distance. (See figure 5-9.) Usually a throw or

5-9. THROWING THE BALL INTO PLAY

A: Underhanded for accuracy.   **B:** Overhead for power and distance.

punt to the opposite side of the field from which the ball came will find less of a crowd and should be the first choice considered. The goalie should never feel rushed. It is important to never throw the ball to the center of the field into the teeth of the other team's attack.

Punting is more difficult. However, if nearby teammates are marked, a punt is the best option. (See figure 5-10 on page 82.) To punt, the goalie should do the following:

1. Face the location or player she wants to punt to.
2. Bend forward, holding the ball in the palm of the left hand (for a right-footed kick), cradling or guiding it gently with the right hand. (Do the opposite for a left-footed kick.)
3. Still bending and with her head down, take two quick steps—a short step with the right foot and a larger leaping step with the left foot.
4. Holding the ball low, still bending forward, and facing slightly to the right of the target, softly lob the ball to the place where the kicking foot will meet it—not too high. Let it travel in the air as short a distance as possible.
5. Lock the kicking foot, and strike the ball hard and explosively with the instep, directly on the shoelaces. Look at the point of the ball, underside about one-fourth of the way up from the bottom, where contact will be made. Leg speed is essential.
6. Follow through fully and gracefully; the body will pull the plant foot forward into a hop.
7. Practice, practice, practice.

The goalie should first look to throw the ball to a teammate who is free. Kicking away leads to a lost possession a higher percentage of the time. However, at younger ages, kids can kick a lot farther than they can throw. Often the coach will just want to get the ball as far away from the goal as possible, particularly when the fullbacks have trouble receiving a goalie pass and controlling the ball. Again, game dynamics depend on the skills of the players. If the team is not skilled, then the coach may choose just to have players kick the ball as far as possible and hope to get lucky.

11. Defending penalty kicks. Often the best defense is to unsettle the kicker. The goalie should take her time, walk around the goal area, and not be in a hurry to get set up. Make the kicker wait. Stare him in the eye. As he goes for the ball, she should sway or feint a bit to one side, opposite to the side you intend to protect. She should first step

5-10. **PUNTING**

A: Hold the ball out, focus on the ball, take two steps.

B: Head down focused on ball, leap to plant foot, lob ball to point of contact.

C: Lock angle, snap into ball with foot speed and follow through.

out a bit and then drive to the side. Usually the ball travels low to the ground, so the goalie must be ready to reach far and low.

GOALIE DRILLS

1. Play catch. The best practice and warm up for goalies is simply to play catch. Two goalies should work together throwing the ball to each other, first sitting, then kneeling, then standing. Throw hard, varying the throw to the sides, high, and low.

2. Striker madness. Two forwards with balls spread out in the penalty box and alternatively take turns shooting goals. Once a shot is taken, the goalie returns the ball to the shooter, and then the other forward shoots. Shots must be two-touch pass, a small dribble and a shot. This gives the goalie time to get into position, but shooters shouldn't wait for full positioning, since you want the goalie to hustle.

3. Breakaway. Two forwards line up outside the penalty box and alternately attack the goal. The goalie starts from the correct position (on the arc described on page 76) and charges the attacker. After the shot, the forward retrieves the ball, and the other forward initiates her attack.

4. Up 'n Over. The coach stands 10–15 feet from the goalie and firmly throws balls at the crossbar. The goalie must decide whether to catch it, let it go, or push it over the bar. Throw from side to side.

05

OFFENSE AND DEFENSE 06

FORMATIONS

Twenty years ago, most American youth teams played a 4-3-3 formation: four fullbacks, three halfbacks, and three forwards (and of course the goalie). The common approach these days is a more defensive 4-4-2, in effect dropping one forward position in favor of an additional halfback. The 4-4-2 formation emphasizes defense. The four defenders play in a diamond shape, with a sweeper who will defensively sweep the ball away from the area in front of the goal, playing behind the center fullback, (or stopper) on the defensive line. The stopper will usually mark the opposition center forward. The four halfbacks will play in a line across midfield, but are quite mobile, with the outside halfbacks ready to penetrate up to the wing and into the corner on attack.

There are many variations on this, depending on the abilities of the players, game conditions, and the other team's approach. Some teams will use different formations depending on the strengths or weaknesses of their opponent. A team with a very good stopper can afford to go with three defenders, adding a position to the midfield or forward lines.

Over the past ten years most youth soccer associations across the country have adopted rules that call for fewer players and for playing on smaller fields. The recommendations of U.S. Youth Soccer are for teams of three to eight players each on the field, increasing in size from ages four to eleven. At age twelve and above, teams of eleven per side are recommended. While many clubs have limited team size, they often still allow for teams slightly larger than recommended by national rules. For instance, as I write this edition, my granddaughter plays on a U10 team that fields eight players in a game on a field 80 yards in length, as opposed to the recommendation for seven players on a field 45–60 yards long. It is abundantly clear to me that the smaller team and field are preferable. The larger team and field still promote too much swarm soccer.

Next year she will move to eleven per side, instead of the eight players recommended for U12. Far too large. I hope all clubs soon will fully adopt U.S. Soccer rules.

SMALL-SIDED GAMES

Beginner Levels

At beginner levels, with teams of three to five players, usually without a goalie, formations are pretty irrelevant. The small-sided game fields are quite small, which reduces the relevance of positioning. Very young kids have great difficulty grasping field positions anyway.

In a three-on-three game, most formations have a sweeper and two forwards. The idea is to have one good player know that he should stay back a bit, or get back quickly when needed. In a four-on-four game, the coach can try a diamond 1-2-1, which I like much better than a 2-2 box. The kids are loosely responsible for an area and need to keep an eye on that area if they move forward with the ball, gravitating back toward their designated spot when they can. Again, the key is to find a defensive-minded stopper who will protect the goal area. We know that positions and formations are nearly irrelevant on such a small game; however, the basic idea of keeping at least one player always behind the ball as a stopper is the best approach.

Defense in small-sided games is a blend of man-to-man and zone. On transition, when the other team gets possession, the stopper must pick up any forward, and the other players must mark the opponent closest to them and stay with him. The key in small games is to quickly transition from offense to defense. Defense must be passive, since there is generally no rear support and a missed tackle will likely lead to a goal. Defenders should drop back until a safe opportunity is available to tackle the ball.

Goal kicks are very important, so teams should have a few set plays available. Stand the sweeper (since there is no goalie) a few feet behind the ball on the goal line, while the other two or three players line up 10 feet away. Upon the sweeper's move, each player breaks away, one to the sideline, one upfield, and the other (if its four on four) to the opposite side. Which player goes in which direction depends on the play called by the sweeper. The three options can be numbered (1, 2, or 3) and the sweeper can call out the number. After the pass, the sweeper should quickly move to cover the goal area. Direct, corner, and sideline kicks are to be done very quickly before the opponent can mark up. The main practice strategy for such small-sided games is to play, play, play. The kids will learn how to play creatively. Also, kids should shoot, shoot, shoo, whenever they can.

Be sure to substitute frequently. Kids need a break after a few minutes.

Intermediate Levels

At intermediate levels, U10 or U12, teams will field seven or eight players including the goalie. Field formations become more meaningful, particularly at U12. The most popular formation for seven players on the field is the 2-3-1, and 3-2-2 is the best when eight take the field. These are easiest to learn. Keep your strength on defense, and modify from that posture depending on what your players show they can do.

Even with these smaller fields and teams, the presence of forwards, halfbacks, and fullbacks in formations with seven or eight players allows for the full range of offensive concepts to be taught. Kids are doing fine, especially at U10 levels, if the players can stay reasonably close to their designated areas while still taking some opportunities to move forward or drop back when needed. It's important to work on halfback positioning. Halfbacks tend to join the forward line or drop back too far on defense, leaving no one in the midfield. You will often see groups on the forward line, and another group back in defense, separated too far to be of help to each other. Find halfbacks who will understand their role and place.

Keep playing four-on-four games in practice at this level to teach the kids how to solve problems and rely on their skills. Don't agonize over whether you have the right formation. The focus is always skill development at youth-level play, and it is skills that eventually allow for separation of the swarm.

As to game strategy, soccer is much less programmed and choreographed than American football, where each play is carefully diagrammed and players are to follow the play patterns closely. Soccer is a fluid game, and players have the opportunity to be much more creative and must decide on their own what to do in each situation. Soccer depends upon the dynamics and opportunities of the moment.

This is not to say that there are no plays or overall strategies in soccer. There clearly are both. However, soccer strategy involves a system of concepts that are applied in given situations. These concepts should be discussed during breaks and at any team meetings.

TOP EIGHT OFFENSIVE CONCEPTS

1. Attack from the wings. We already touched on this concept in chapter five when discussing the forward wing position. The basic idea is to get the ball as far forward as possible. Moving it through the wing, or corner areas, is the easiest way because the defense is usually stronger up the middle than it is on the wing. You can never overstate this concept to your team. The offside rule means that offensive ground must be earned by the ball, so dribbling the ball and penetrating well into the wing or corner allows the other forwards to advance laterally to the goal, staying even with the advance of the ball. (See again figure 5-2 on page 69.)

In setting up a wing attack, the halfbacks or center forward must get the ball to a wing forward. The pass to the wing depends on timing and will improve with practice and experience. Usually, it is best to pass the ball well ahead of the wing forward who can then run up to it, particularly if the wing area has open space free of defenders. This allows the wing forward to sprint past her defender, retrieve the ball, advance it, and then center the ball, that is, execute a pass to the striker in front of the goal.

The wing forward should move the ball as close to the goal line as possible before centering the ball out in front of the goal. If the defender can be beaten, the forward can angle toward the goal for a shot. Otherwise, angle for the corner and plan the move that will set up a good centering pass. As stated earlier, the striker cannot penetrate further upfield than the ball because of the offside rule. Therefore, if the wing gets the ball near the goal line, the striker will be able to get directly in front of the goal to receive the centering pass. Often, the wing can pass the ball to himself, that is, kick it into open space in the corner area and run up to it. This works often, since the corner area is usually undefended.

2. Spread the field. The best offense is one that stretches the field, creating a lot of space for passes or dribbling. The antithesis of the swarm soccer we see with kids is having players spread wide apart. It takes years to get kids to move from a *chase the ball* mentality to one that has them asking "Where do I need to be to get a pass or to support the dribbler?" By running up close to a teammate with the ball, a kid often just gets in the way or, worse, brings another defender with him and thus adds pressure on the dribbler.

The best way to coach field position is to run scrimmages and continually stop play, telling everyone to freeze with the whistle. Then talk about where people are and where they should be. For instance, if someone has the ball along the sideline, there should be someone heading to support him, behind him a bit, in case he loses the ball. There should be someone ahead or to the side looking for open space to get a pass. Players assigned to the other side of the field should be wide, looking for a cross pass (discussed below), but not so wide that they are out of range to receive a pass.

Defensive players tend to flow with the ball and gravitate toward it. Therefore, a very effective offensive strategy is to boot the ball across the field to the opposite side, catching defenders off balance and out of position, and allowing a teammate open space to advance the ball. This requires a pretty strong foot, but the fields are narrower in youth play, so it still can be done. This also requires that a player stay wide and away from defenders on the opposite side of the field so she can be open for such a pass.

Offensive players on the opposite side of the field often tend to creep toward the side where the ball is. Wing forwards especially can't allow this to happen. They must always stay wide. There is usually much open space along the opposite sideline, so you need the wing forwards to stay wide for any pass, from any angle, which will allow them to get the ball and then penetrate into their corner. Staying wide also will pull a defender from the middle and open up that area a bit. (See figure 6-1.) Often, a player with the ball won't see that a wing is free for a cross pass, and someone may need to help him. You will often hear someone yell out "cross," and that means that a wing is open across the field.

A *cross pass* is a powerful offensive weapon. It catches defenders by surprise, and leads to breakaway attacks, or deep penetration into the corner area. Many easy goals are scored off such situations. Of course, as noted, it requires a strong foot, so it is not seen often at younger ages. Have players stay wide, but not so wide they cannot be reached.

6-1. WINGS STAY WIDE FOR CROSSING PASS

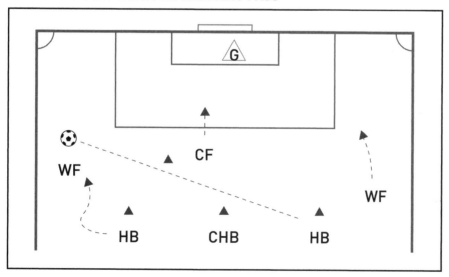

As defenders bunch toward the ball, a long crossing pass to the opposite wing can be a powerful play, catching the defense by surprise. This is why wings must stay wide.

3. Overlap and support. Earlier we talked about field positions. Some players attack, some defend, some work at midfield transition. Many youth coaches will tell their players not to cross midfield if they are defenders, or not to come back past midfield if they are forwards, that right halfbacks don't go on the left side of the field, and the like. "Play your position!" Well, the coach may be trying to impress upon the team that they do have the primary responsibility for their section of the field, but seizing an opportunity to dribble the ball upfield when the path is wide open, thus overlapping into another more forward position, is an essential part of soccer. Players need to be able to take advantage of such opportunities to advance the ball.

The concept of overlap is that a player, with or without the ball, can move past a teammate in front, or to the side, if it creates a favorable offensive condition. If a player moves out of position, then other players need to adjust, and provide support to the now vacated position by filling in, rotating, and otherwise ensuring that the overall defensive positioning is sound. The overlapped player may need to drop back, or another player may fill in. Players need to know how to fill in for each other and how to back each other up. The concept requires some experience. This is why youth coaches worry about overlaps—the kids aren't always experienced enough to back each other up, leaving a gaping hole in the defense. However, players need to understand the concept, and to know that some day soon, they will be expected to overlap, or even to change positions, just to confuse the defense. (See figure 6-2 on page 91.) The coach can always yell out "carry" when a player has room to advance and overlap, and then "support" when overlapping causes a defensive vulnerability, thus signaling others to look to fill in.

4. Move off the ball. When players are *off the ball*, meaning they are not handling the ball, they must decide where they are most needed. This involves creating open spaces, lending support, and setting up plays. They never just stand and watch; that's what fans are for. This concept is called *moving off the ball*. (See figure 6-3 on page 92.) Players generally should spread out and move with the flow of the ball, upfield, downfield, right, or left. That's easy and natural. If they are behind the ball, they should probably move to support the dribbler, help out if they lose the ball, or be available for a pass back. However, if near or upfield of the ball, players must get into position to receive the ball. Now, this is done so long as the teammate with the ball can get a pass off. There is no sense running to an open spot if the ball carrier can't see or reach the receiver. Players without the ball are also expected to feint and fake, to get their defenders to lean one way so they can then dart the other way for a pass.

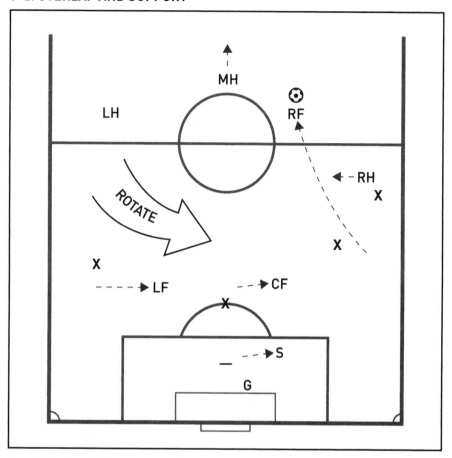

The right fullback (RF) sees an open field and dribbles the ball upfield. The other fullbacks and sweeper then rotate toward the undefended area, and the overlapped right halfback (RH) fills in for immediate support.

5. Create open space. Moves off the ball are often designed to create open space. This advanced concept requires maturity and experience. The idea is that a player creates an open space by leaving an area and taking a defender with him. This allows a player to dribble or pass to the area that is now open. For example, if a wing forward sees a halfback with the ball begin to dribble past his own defender, the wing should move away, taking the wing's defender with him, so the halfback can freely dribble further upfield.

91

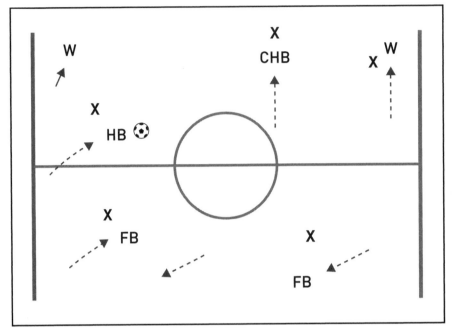

Halfback with ball moves away from defender (X). Fullback trails play in case HB loses ball. Center halfback sets up for a give and go. Wings move up for a corner pass. Everyone is involved in movement off ball.

Another way to create open space is to do a *switch*. To do a switch, two players who are both off the ball, such as a wing forward and center forward, simply switch positions. The wing forward cuts toward the center of the field, leaving what is now an open space, and the center forward heads to this open wing area to receive a pass from midfield. If it works, open space will be created at least momentarily both in the wing and at the center forward area for both switching players. (See figure 6-4 on page 93.) Now a halfback with the ball has a triangle, and possibly two options for a pass. This play works best when the defense is marking both players very closely, instead of defending areas. It confuses the defense momentarily, allowing the striker a step to get open, receive a pass, advance the ball, and make a move, such as centering the ball back to the wing forward or the halfback attacking the goal.

Fullbacks are generally not called upon to create space, but need to position themselves in a good area to support a dribbler and be open for a possible safety pass from a halfback in trouble. Their job is to back up the player with the ball if it is on their

6-4. CREATE OPEN SPACE

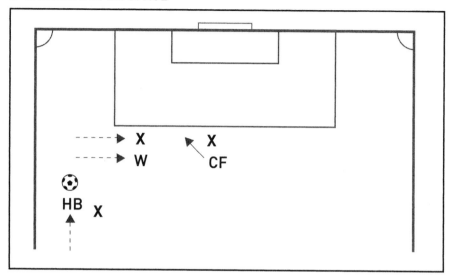

Thsi is not an easy concept for kids to apply. Here the wing moves toward the center of the field, taking defender (X) with her. The halfback with the ball is then free to dribble to the open space created by the wing's move. The center forward then moves or angles for a center pass

side of the field. Also, if an opponent takes the ball away, a fullback needs to be close by to challenge the new attack. The other fullbacks must quickly position themselves to support and defend against a possible breakaway if the ball gets by the first fullback. This is called *slanting*, and will be covered more when we talk about defensive strategy. It basically means the defender stays in the backfield well behind the ball.

6. Triangulation. Ultimately, particularly at youth levels where very long kicks are not yet possible, soccer comes down to three teammates working together in most situations: the player with the ball and the two closest to her, usually one to her side and one in front of her. This is why kids start with three-on-three soccer, one with the ball, one who is in the best position for a pass, and the third player moving off the ball, looking to create the next play or to support the other two. At all times, these players form a triangle, and thinking of themselves as part of a triangle is conducive to their playing as a unit.

One key to the triangulation offense is the wall pass, which I prefer to call the give-and-go play. It's so simple, and yet for some reason kids often don't look for it. They pass the ball to a teammate (just getting them to pass takes time), and then they stop. The moment of a pass is the best time to shake a defender. Often the defender is off balance looking at the passed ball. Players might also slow down when the pass is made, figuring their job is done. The trick is to take advantage of the defender's momentary pause. (See figure 6-5.)

When players pass the ball, they should break upfield in the same motion to get away from the defender and also help the receiver to notice that he is breaking free. The receiver then passes the ball back. This is also called a *wall pass*, because the first receiver one-touches it back, like the ball rebounding on a wall. It's simple. Give the ball to a teammate and go get the return pass. It works a high percentage of the time, and I am surprised that it is used so little. It is useful in older age levels, where the game is more open, but in youth soccer where the game is much closer, it is a powerful play. Talk about this concept with your players and practice it. Let your young player kick the ball to you and then dash ahead for a return pass. The key is in breaking forward at the same time as passing the ball.

Another example of a triangle play is the *square pass*. Teams primarily seek to advance the ball and almost never pass the ball to the center of the field in front of their own goal. That's exactly where the opposition wants the ball. However, a pass

6–5. **WALL PASS: GIVE AND GO**

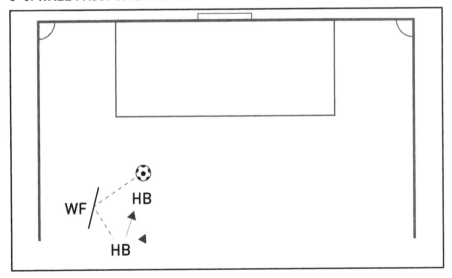

The give-and-go or wall pass: The halfback passes to the wing forward and dashes upfield for the return pass.

to the center is a viable option when the wings are covered and there is no room for dribbling. In this case, a halfback who is free will run up the middle to the side of the player under pressure and yell out "square," which tells him to pass the ball laterally to the middle. (See figure 6-6.) The player with the ball may not have seen the teammate at his side, so it helps to have someone yell out. The passer and his support then move up with the pass, creating a triangle for the halfback who received the pass.

Triangle drill: Remember the triangle passing drill (from page 43)? It's really designed for the triangle unit to practice offense. Set up four cones in a square about 10 yards apart. Three players with one ball stand next to a cone. The player with the ball passes it to one of the other two, and then quickly runs to the open cone. The receiver does likewise, passing to one of the two, and running to the now vacant cone, and so forth. New triangles are set up with each play. After a while the coach goes to the middle and applies mild pressure, blocking one of the two passing lanes. Finally, the coach should apply full pressure, really trying to get the ball.

7. Make things happen. The lack of choreographed plays is soccer's great distinction from other major sports. Players are free to determine what opportunities are available

6–6. **SQUARE**

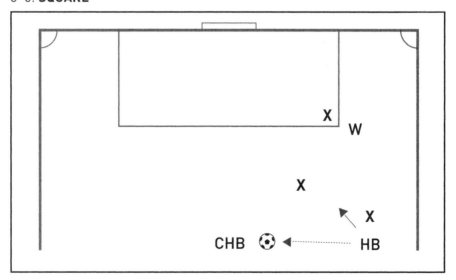

Here the halfback with the ball cannot advance, so the center halfback yells "square," thus calling for a lateral pass.

and use their creativity to react to a dynamic situation and make things happen. Forwards and halfbacks should be encouraged to take good shots. Yell out positive phrases like "good try," "keep shooting," or "nice shot." Obviously, players need to learn to stay away from bad shots, but the general approach must be a positive one. They can't score if they don't shoot. Often, young players get the ball and pass too quickly. If no defender is nearby, players must try to advance the ball. First, it gets the ball farther upfield; and second, it forces a defender to come to the ball, away from any potential receiver. If no one is pressuring the ball, teammates should yell, "carry it," or "push it." This tells the dribbler that no one is approaching from behind. When a defender does approach, yell out "man on," which signals that it's time to pass.

8. Communicate. The chatter among players must be constant. The coaches need to teach players in practice to communicate with each other, or it won't happen during games. The primary calls are:

"Carry:" There is room to dribble.

"Cross" or "switch:" Pass across the field.

"Support:" A teammate is supporting behind the player if needed.

"Leave it:" Don't touch the ball, someone else has a better play.

"Man on:" Pressure is very close behind.

"Through:" Pass the ball between two defenders to a teammate running off the ball.

"Time:" There is time to assess options; no pressure near.

"1-2:" Make a wall pass.

There are more calls in the glossary, but make sure these eight are used when they should be.

TOP NINE DEFENSIVE CONCEPTS

As with many sports, defense is largely a matter of reacting. The offense sets the play into motion, and the defense needs to react and defend accordingly.

Most American youth teams will build their team from the back forward, keeping the defense strong, and employing a sweeper to mark an exceptional opposing player. Soccer is viewed largely as a defensive game. Scores are low because of this.

1. Challenge the ball. Often at youth levels we see a kid dribble a long way with no one putting any pressure on her. We often hear coaches screaming, "Someone get her! Go to the ball!" The closest defender, often called the first defender, must get quickly to the dribbler to avoid giving up too much ground. Whatever the case, someone *must* go after the dribbler.

Also, defenders are expected to deny passing lanes to the player they are marking and tackle the ball before the opponent has control. We touched on this in chapter four. The best time to attack players with the ball is just as they are trapping it, before they get full control, keeping in mind that the first priority is to stay between the ball and the goal.

2. Contain and apply pressure, but don't overcommit. The essence of soccer defense is pressure. The goal is to slow down and contain the offense—to prohibit offensive players from getting past a defender with the ball and to pressure the ball carrier into making a mistake. This is especially true if there is no defensive support close behind. One might think the main idea is to *get* the ball, and that is certainly one objective. But the primary objective is for players to protect the field behind them, stay between the ball and the goal, and apply pressure.

Defenders often overcommit by rushing the ball, only to have the dribbler slip by. They must learn to be patient, maintain their balance, and try to get the offensive player to commit first. The best way to regain possession is to force a mistake or a bad pass, and then get to the ball. I tell the kids to pretend they are going to charge, feint, or fake a step, and then see if the dribbler commits. Sometimes just the presence of a defender will cause a player to kick the ball away and lose possession. The defender should be close enough to apply pressure, but not so close that the dribbler can sweep by. If the dribbler hesitates long enough, another defender may be able to provide support. When two defenders double team a player, the second defender to arrive tackles the ball.

It is important for a defender to try to use the whole body to trap the ball. At young ages in particular, the child will stick out a toe or thigh to a moving ball and miss it completely. If there is time, the player should try to get in front of the ball, and trap it fully with the side of the foot, or with the body if the ball is in the air. This will minimize missing the ball completely.

To summarize, the defender's job is to stop forward progress of the player with the ball, apply pressure, and avoid going too quickly for the ball (unless the defender is sure he can get a foot on it). Obviously, a dribbler getting past a defender will penetrate

06

closer to the goal, and this requires another defender to assist (if there is another one between the ball and the goal). We covered tackling in chapter five, and it should be reviewed again.

3. Cover and support. Once the offense loses possession, the players must immediately transition back to defense. The concept commonly used here is to *shift and sag*, which means to shift to a position between the ball and the goal, and to sag or fall back to set up layers of defense. While the first defender to the ball must pressure the opponent, being cautious not to let the ball get by him, the job of the second defender is to provide support by covering the area 15–25 feet behind the first defender. This layer should yell out "support" to indicate her presence, thus allowing the first defender to be more aggressive in trying to tackle the opponent. The second defender then needs to mark any opponents in the area and try to deny any pass to them by positioning herself in the passing lane. (See figure 6-7 on page 99.) Other defenders should look to provide deeper cover. This entails trying to anticipate where the play will head by observing the field and looking for opportunities available to the offense, marking players, and filling in any open space.

4. Keep the ball away from the middle. If the ball is along the sideline, especially if past midfield toward the defense's goal, the defender's job is to ensure that the dribbler does not penetrate toward the center of the field. The defensive objective is to continue to force the player with the ball to stay wide, along the sidelines. The defender tries to gain possession and also tries to get in the way of any centering pass. Once again, players should be more concerned with keeping the attacker away and under control than tackling. They should tackle the ball only when they are certain they will be successful, and only when another defender is supporting the move.

Good offense tries to advance the ball up the sideline and then pass to the middle in front of the penalty area. Therefore, good defense tries to prevent the centering pass from happening. To do this when defending an opponent who has either just received the ball or stopped to prepare for a centering pass, defenders take a stance called *side on*, with the front foot pointing toward the ball and the back foot pointing toward the sideline, knees bent and weight low and forward, allowing for quick reflexive action. The front foot is positioned to defend against dribbling or passing into the middle, and the back foot positions the body to defend any further move down the sideline.

On another note regarding the middle, fullbacks must be reminded when *clearing* a ball, that is, booting it away from the goal area (see number seven on page

6-7. **COVER AND SUPPORT**

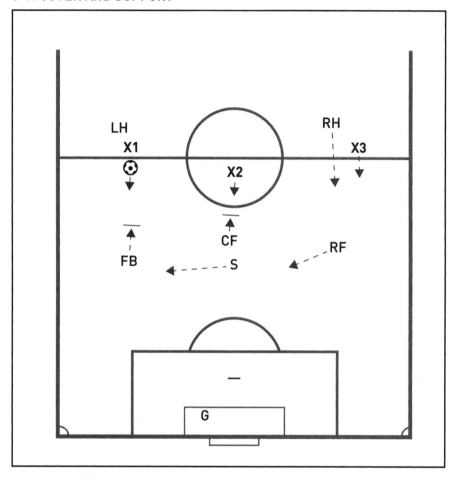

First defender (FB) covers the ball and contains until second defender (S) provides support. Third (X3) and other defenders balance the defense.

101)—to kick it to the side and never to the middle. An opponent may trap it and shoot at the goal.

5. Marking. A basic defensive strategy is to mark or cover players in a defender's zone, to keep an eye on them. A defender should be able to anticipate a pass to such an opponent and intercept it, or otherwise be near enough and in position to pressure her. Sometimes, the defender's presence alone will prevent the pass. Tell your players to try to think where the pass will go and get into position to intercept it if in their zone. In front of the goal, unmarked players will often score; they *must* all be marked, and in this case, the marking must be very close. The best position for marking is between the player and the goal, slightly on the ball side of the player, about 2 to 3 feet from the player.

6. Offside trap. This is an important concept. Offside, as defined in chapter one, essentially means that forwards can't hang around the goal waiting for a pass. There are only two ways that an offensive player can advance toward the goal: 1) if the ball is closer to the goal than the player is; or 2) if a defensive player other than the goalie is closer to the goal than the offensive player. Therefore, it makes a lot of sense for defensive players not to hang around the goal. If they do, offensive players can do so also. Fullbacks on their half of the field want to stay as far upfield as they can, knowing that the forwards on the opposing team can't advance farther than their position without the ball. Of course, the defensive players must fall back as the ball approaches or passes their line, since everybody may always advance at least as far as the ball. Therefore, once the ball is played back upfield, fullbacks will yell, "Move out," head upfield, and force forwards to withdraw with them.

Another defensive strategy is to use the offside rule to gain possession of the ball. A fullback downfield of the ball can run up past the person she is guarding, and as soon as that person affects the play (e.g., a pass is made to him), the referee will blow the whistle, call offside, and award possession to the defense. The team receiving possession gets a free indirect kick. Fullbacks must make sure another fullback isn't also behind the opposing player or the trap will not work.

Often teams will call an offside trap, wherein a designated player calls the trap and all fullbacks run forward past the offensive players. This is usually done just before an opponent passes the ball forward, resulting in an offside penalty. (See figure 6-8 on page 101.)

Of course, offside traps can be quite dangerous. If the defensive player does not get past the offensive player before the ball is kicked, then the offensive player may have a free strike on the goal. Or, the referee may miss the offside penalty. In youth soccer, where there is usually only one field referee and no linesmen, this occurs frequently, to a chorus of groans from parents and fans. Many a game has been decided on a missed offside call. Players should learn to raise their hands upon an offside to get the referee's attention. It's often hard to see these penalties from a distance. I like to have all fullbacks raise their hands on an offside trap, so the referee is alerted. In any event, the players must keep playing if they don't hear a whistle.

6-8. OFFSIDE TRAP

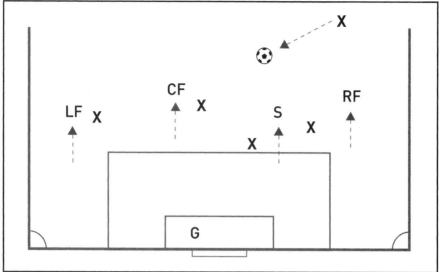

Before X plays the ball, all fullbacks and the sweeper, on signal, suddenly advance upfield. Then, as soon as the ball is passed, the opponent closest to the goal is offside.

7. Clear when in trouble. A fullback who has just gained possession, but with no good passing or dribbling option, must get the ball away from the goal, even if it means kicking it out of bounds. This at least allows the defense to reform and protect the goal. Players should not hesitate to kick the ball out of bounds if in any doubt at all about being able to safely pass it upfield. This hard defensive kick clears the ball from the area in front of the goal. Another option is to pass back to the goalie, if he is not too far away. This is a form of safety pass. However, if there is any chance an opposing player can intercept, the ball should not be passed. Remember, it's a pass, not a shot. Make it firm and direct but not too hard. I've seen goals scored on this play. I've seen the safety pass get by the goalie and roll into the net. However, it can be a very effective defensive play. The goalie can then punt or pass the ball to an open teammate.

It's essential to not kick into an opposing player. This will happen and is sometimes hard to avoid. It's deadly when a fullback does it. I've also seen goals scored because a fullback kicked a ball into a striking forward, who rebounded it unintentionally right into the net. Tell your players to try to pass the ball around any opposing player.

8. Make a wall. Upon certain penalties, as discussed in chapter one, the referee will award a free direct or indirect kick. If the kick is taken from near the penalty area, there is a good chance to score, so the defense needs to mak a human wall to help the goalie. In youth soccer this is often a confused process, but there is no need for it to be.

The wall protects against shots directed at the near-post goal area, and the goalie covers the far-post area. The goalie calls out how many players are needed in the wall based on the conditions of the kick. Shots near the line marking the penalty area require five players in the wall, and the number drops as distance or angle to the goal increases. The wall is usually made up of the center fullback, the wing fullback on the side the kick is coming from, the sweeper, the wing halfback, and the center halfback. One person, usually the center fullback, is the *wall captain*. This person is responsibile to organize the wall and shift it based on the goalie's instructions. The wall captain raises a number of fingers, based on the goalie's instruction, to call for the number of players in the wall. The captain lines up in line with the near post, and the other players line up on the captain's inside shoulder. Players all have assigned numbers and positions in the wall, and line up accordingly. If the captain raises four fingers, then the defenders assigned number two, three, or four join the captain on the line. (See figure 6-9.) The wall must be at least 10 yards from the ball.

6-9. **MAKE A WALL**

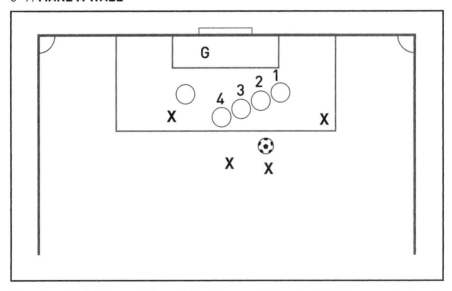

The wall captain (1) lines up between ball and near post. Since the ball is dangerously close he calls for a four-man wall, and the players with assigned numbers line up in order.

It's essential to form walls quickly; they should be practiced. The offense will try to get the shot off before the wall is formed. Other players who could receive a short pass on the free kick must be marked, and the goalie must ensure that no opponent is unmarked. For the small-sided games in youth soccer, the walls are smaller. In three on three, play the wall as a single person; in four on four, play two in the wall, standing about 4 yards away. For games of seven or eight on a side, the wall should be three or four players standing not closer than 8 yards from the ball. As a general rule, walls should comprise about half of the field of players.

9. Communicate. As with offensive communication—perhaps even more importantly—defenders must communicate. This must occur at practice, since kids need to learn how and when to communicate to their teammates. The key terms for defense are:

"Clear:" The ball handler is in trouble and should kick the ball out of bounds.

"Help him:" Someone needs to provide support for a defender.

"Mark up:" There are undefended players, usually around the penalty box.

"Make a wall:" There is a direct kick near the penalty box; look at the goalie and see how many are needed in the wall.

"Two:" You have two players and need some help.

"Hold her:" Delay the dribbler until support can arrive.

"Keeper:" The goalie is saying he can get the ball, so leave it alone. (This can only be called out by the goalie.)

RUNNING TEAM PRACTICE 07

A major factor in a team's improvement during a season is the organization of the coach. Practices can be very effective in improving skills, soccer savvy, and teamwork. However, an unorganized practice can leave kids standing around, wasting precious time and learning opportunities. Organization must start even before the season. Coaches must be prepared, get parents involved, and inform all team members of what to expect. Then, once practice starts, you must be prepared so that you make sure every minute of practice time is being used effectively. Later in this chapter, I'll discuss the idea of having stations at practice. I have found this to be the best method for keeping kids involved throughout an entire practice while also teaching them the most skills possible. In addition to skills stations, don't underestimate the importance of just letting kids play, in small-sided games. Of course, they need to be taught proper form, rules, and specialty skills, and they need to practice ball control such as dribbling, juggling, and trapping. But the way they will become good players is to play the game. Too often, coaches spend too much time in instruction and too little in game dynamics.

PRESEASON PREPARATION

The coaching job starts on day one—before the season even begins. A month or so before the first practice, you should communicate with your team, as well as with the parents, on a number of matters. Suggest to parents that their child will have a much easier start if she shows up in decent shape. Soccer doesn't require the strength of some other sports, but it does require endurance, quickness, and agility. It's best, particularly at grade-school levels, if players are able to do six, 25-yard wind sprints and are able to jog four or five laps around the field. This means the kids should work at least every other day for a couple weeks to get up to this level. Parents can jog with their kids and get exercise too.

Players and parents also need to know that practices are important, and that being on time is important for them and for the team. The game schedule, practice schedule, and starting and ending times all should be communicated when they are available, so the players can begin arranging for transportation and free up their calendar.

You should also communicate that you welcome help. At least two assistant coaches are needed; three or four is better. A team "parent" or two is needed to help with incidentals: uniforms, candy drives, organizing car pools, bringing refreshments to games, and the like. Ask for help. Here is a sample letter to parents:

and I recommend you obtain it. I also need a team parent or two to help organize things. If you are interested, give me a call or see me at the first practice.

My philosophy is to help your child learn the skills and fundamentals of the game, and become better at, and have fun with the great game of soccer. Most kids do not go on to play at professional levels, but if they learn the basics, they will enjoy the game their whole lives. Every child will play in each half of every game (state the league rule about minimum playing time). Those who work harder may get some additional playing time, but they must earn it. Winning is fun, but it is not as important as making this a positive learning experience. (If your league does not even keep score at this age, say so.)

I hope you will keep this in mind when rooting for the team or your child at games. It's helpful to praise good hustle and effort, but not helpful to give specific instructions to your child during play (that's my role) or to comment on referee calls (they are learning, too). I will not allow criticism from parents or from other players.

It is most helpful for parents to work with their child at home to improve skills. Encourage dribbling, juggling, and trapping. Practice definitely leads to improvement, so more is always better. A little one on one will also help (and gives you some exercise, too). Encourage kids to get together for small backyard games, two on two, or three on three.

Of course, if your schedule does not permit all of the above, you have already taken a big step by allowing your child to be involved and by providing transportation. Welcome aboard!

Best Regards,

Coach Jack McCarthy
Phone number, e-mail, address

TEACH THE LANGUAGE OF SOCCER

Don't assume your players, especially beginners, know what you are talking about when you mention specific soccer skills or techniques. Kids need to learn the basics of the game, and you need to start by defining what they are. For beginners, it's good during breaks at practice to call the team together and spend a few minutes on soccer talk. Have a few new words each practice and ask the kids who knows what they mean. Start with the basic stuff—parts of the field, rules, and positions. Make it fun, and use the opportunity to elaborate on the meaning of things.

FIND EXTRA PRACTICE TIME

Unfortunately, you will not get as much practice time for your team as you want or need. Clinics for beginners play once or twice a week. Club teams may practice twice and play on weekends. School teams may practice more regularly. Many teams seek access to fields, so they often must be shared by many. Fields are often wet and unusable. Yet, an enterprising coach can find creative ways to get more practice time. Clearly, the best practice condition is on a regulation field, but any grassy area will do for dribbling and passing, as well as for small-sided games. Videotape scrimmages and plan an evening at someone's house to view them, maybe with some pizza. There are many ways to gain additional practice, even if it's only to urge mom and dad, or big brother or sister, to spend thirty minutes passing or mildly pressuring a player while dribbling. Advise parents about shortcomings in their child's form so they can help make needed changes. The more you get your players drilling their skills, within reason, the better your team will be. That's the surest thing about any sport. Sure, you may not be able to spend every night practicing, but that's where parents and assistant coaches come in.

INDOOR SOCCER

I placed this section in this chapter since most coaches view indoor soccer as off-season practice, a way to have fun, play a faster moving game, and hone skills. It can be a great way to get extra practice time. I don't mean this to lessen the sport at all, and my teams had great times in indoor play, especially when playing in an official indoor rink with synthetic turf fields. Most indoor play is in a school gymnasium, and is still a lot of fun as well as good experience for kids who want to play during the winter. (See figure 7-1 on page 109).

There is an official indoor soccer association governing the sport nationally, the United States Indoor Soccer Association, found at *www.usindoor.com*. Their rules call for teams of five to seven players, including a goalie, for teams under twelve years of age. Games are in two (running-clock) halves with free substitutions. Free kicks replace throw-ins. Long or high kicks are fouls; the idea is to play a controlled game and keep the ball low. Some leagues give out time penalties, as in ice hockey, for certain fouls. Look into indoor opportunities in your area and get your players involved.

7-1. INDOOR SOCCER

Great winter practice, quick pace, lots of fun!

SET YOUR PRACTICE GOALS

Soccer practices typically last an hour and a half, depending on the day of the week and the amount of daylight. Coaches need to set their goals for practices at the outset.

In a ninety minute practice, I would devote ten minutes to chatter and water breaks, ten minutes to warm-ups, thirty minutes to skills development, and forty or more minutes to game condition scrimmages and team dynamics. You can do a few things at the same time. In fact, if you have many parent-coaches helping out you can seemingly double these time frames.

Early in the season you should spend a bit more time on conditioning, speed, and agility drills. Later in the season you need to spend more time on specialty drills. Let's look at each goal.

GOAL ONE: GET THE PLAYERS IN SHAPE

Frankly, it doesn't take much to get grade-school kids into shape, and there is just no excuse when they aren't. Soccer requires much endurance, and a lot of improvement can come from some speed and agility drills. The worst mistake is to assume that kids will get themselves into shape. Soccer coaches tend to underestimate the value of conditioning, but stronger kids run longer.

Warming Up

For a non-contact sport, soccer has a lot of injuries. This is due to sudden jerking movements, getting kicked, and collisions. Many injuries can be avoided by warm-up exercises and proper conditioning.

I would suggest avoiding weight training at young ages, at least until high-school age. Jogging, wind sprints, calisthenics (push ups, partial knee bends, sit-ups, neck bridges) are quite sufficient. There is one weight exercise I like that is called the extension lift. It's a mechanism attached to a bench press machine that allows a person in a seated position to extend a bent leg up and straight with weight. Use only enough weigh so that three repetitions of fifteen can be done. This exercise increases kicking strength.

Make sure players warm up before practice. They should get there a few minutes early. A few laps around the field at a slow pace should break a sweat and warm up major leg muscles. Of special concern early in the season are the large muscles high on the inner thigh and in the groin area. Muscles are like bubble gum—unless they stretch slowly they will tear. After stretching, the kids should pair up and pass to each other to loosen up their legs and ankles.

Don't expect that players will warm up sufficiently on their own. They should be told to stretch on their own before practice, but then get the team together to do it some more. Players get hurt too easily when they're not loose, and it's your responsibility to see that they are.

Exercises

Start the team off with what I call the Quick Cali Set: twenty jumping jacks, ten push ups, fifteen half sit-ups, and twenty trunk turns. Then do a few exercises from the Leg Stretch Set. Leg stretches should be done smoothly without jerking or straining. Here are a few good ones. (See figure 7-2 on page 111).

LEG STRETCH SET

1. Butterfly groin. One of the best stretches is for the player to sit on the ground and place the soles of the sneakers together, then gently pull the feet in close for fifteen seconds, relax, and pull in again. Do this three to four times.

2. Thigh stretch. Have the player stand with legs outstretched to the side, then lean to one side, and, bending that knee, stretch the opposite thigh muscle.

3. Toe-hand. The player lies on the back with arms stretched outward on the floor, then alternately brings each foot up and over to the opposite hand.

4. Hurdler. The player sits on the ground with one leg forward, and one bent inward, and touches the forward toe, then switches legs and repeats.

A: Jumping jacks.

B: Cross-legged toe touch.

C: Butterfly groin stretch.

D: Achilles and calf stretch. .

5. Standing quadriceps. Standing on one leg, the player lifts the other foot from behind to touch the buttocks. Do a half dozen for each leg.

6. Supine hamstring. Lying on the back with hands behind one knee, the player pulls that leg, as straight legged as possible, to the chest. He repeats with the other one. No jerking movements, no bobbing up and down.

7. Achilles and calf stretch. The player places one foot in front of the other, leans forward, and bends the front leg, stretching the lower part of the back leg. Then he switches legs.

The team captain, if you have one, or a coach can lead exercises, and you can let him start this part of the practice while you get organized, check to see who is there, or talk to coaches or parents. Monitor your players. Evaluate the heat at all times when doing conditioning, and make sure none of the players gets heat exhaustion.

Don't overwork players. Some coaches have kids running all the time, all season long. The players are young, but there are limits even for the young.

Don't do wind sprints at the beginning of practice. They require the loosest muscles, so do them at the end. Then do short ones, 20 yards at first, then 25 yards. Tell the players to reach out in a long stride. Do some backwards and some sideways. Finish with a few 30-yard races. Wind sprints are essential for leg strength.

Speed Improvement Drills

You can't do much to make a slow kid into the fastest kid on the team, but you can improve speed significantly. You can also improve running strength, agility, and balance.

Some good drills to improve running speed and form are below. The key is to get kids to run on their toes—not flat-footed—and to get their weight—head and shoulders—forward and low. Wind sprints are the best at this. Teach the kids the drills early in the season and encourage them thereafter to do them on their own.

1. The Robot. Line up players and have them run 25–30 yards at half speed, alternately driving their fists down from neck height to just behind the buttocks. The idea is to bang or drive the fists downward in a robotic cadence in rhythm with their stride. Look at track stars in the 100-yard dash and observe how they pump the arms. Have your players run it three times, increasing speed each time.

2. The Bounce. This is similar to the drill above, but players concentrate on lifting their knees high to the chest, bouncing off the ground with each step, lifting the knees as high as possible. This drill is routinely done by track stars and high jumpers. It develops the power thrust needed to sprint. Try to incorporate the first drill with the second after a while, 25–30 yards is fine.

3. The Butt-Kick. Again run 25–30 yards and return, this time kicking the heels into the buttocks. This helps the follow-through needed for a complete stride. Every bit of thrust is needed to sprint.

112

4. The Goosestep. Finally, run 25–30 yards in a goosestep, kicking the legs straight out and lifting them straight and high. The idea here is to train to reach out for a greater stride.

Agility Drills

1. Simon Says. Line up players in three lines. The first row of five starts running in place, in short, quick, choppy steps. The coach signals with his hand for the players to shuffle laterally (without crossing the feet), forward, backward, down to the ground and up again. Players must square the shoulders, stay low and react quickly.

2. Carioca. Lining up as in Simon Says, players do a carioca step, that is, run sideways. The left foot crosses in front of the right, the right foot steps to the right, then the left foot crosses behind the right, and the right foot steps to the right; repeat the pattern for 40 yards. Have players do this drill four times.

GOAL TWO: UNDERSTAND EACH PLAYER'S POTENTIAL

You need to figure out what each player can do, so each can concentrate on developing the specific skills for her position. Then you need to keep an open mind, and, after a while, figure out which players you were wrong about. Many coaches quickly decide who plays where and never change it. But countless times I have seen a coach stick someone in an odd position late in a meaningless game and suddenly find that the kid is a natural there. While it's important to get things set early so you can concentrate on the special skills required for each position (as discussed in chapter five), you should always be looking to see if someone can help the team somewhere else. Assistant coaches can help you here.

A good tool in this respect is to start making lists. Run sprints to see who your fastest players are. Who kicks hard? Who kicks the furthest? Who can accelerate the fastest (short distance speed)? Who are the most agile? Who are the gutsiest players? Who are the best at headers? Who has the best dribbling skills? Once you create these lists, don't throw them away. Check them every couple of weeks to see if someone has earned another look.

The lists force you to evaluate your players according to different aspects of athletic ability. Sometimes you will be surprised to see the name of a player you hadn't been looking at very closely pop up. Constantly evaluate and reevaluate your players. It's incredible to me how rarely some coaches discuss each player. It is far too easy to overlook a quiet kid who may have good ability. An assistant coach usually has seen something that can surface in a full review. Don't label someone for the season.

113

Reconsider constantly. Give a kid a shot at something else if he is not working out where you first placed him.

GOAL THREE: WORK ON INDIVIDUAL SKILLS

After ten minutes of conditioning, stretching, speed and agility drills, I like to call the players together. Tell them generally what they will be doing next and what you expect of them for the next part of practice. Assistant coaches can supply details later. You should focus on individual position skills and fundamentals.

I think it's a great idea to take moving or even still pictures of kids at practice. Try to get a parent to volunteer to take some shots of players working on form—dribbling, passing, trapping. Show the images to kids who need to see what they are doing wrong. You can all meet at someone's house to view films and talk about form. In coaching, as in art, a picture is truly worth a thousand words. Keep it upbeat and constructive.

Working on form and fundamentals is essential. This must start early in the season on a regular basis. Have the checklist found in chapter nine handy to check out form.

PRACTICE STATIONS

I suggest dividing the team into several small groups, or stations, depending on how much help you have. You don't want players daydreaming out in the field during practice.

The practice session will depend on the age of the players. The main variable is how much to focus on skills as opposed to dynamics and field play. At young age levels, more basics are needed. There is no sense in teaching play patterns if kids can't pass or trap.

A key to effective practices is keeping everyone busy. Kids standing in lines waiting their turn to do something is not only wasted time, but also leads to distraction. Divide players into five groups of two or three each and divide the field into as many as five areas or stations, each involving a skill drill. Most days, focus on individual skills, and every so often insert some specialty skills stations.

INDIVIDUAL SKILLS STATIONS

Station 1: Slalom Dribbling—Players weave through a line of cones while dribbling.

Station 2: Trapping—Players throw the ball to each other, at varying heights, forcing use of different body surfaces.

Station 3: Speed Dribbling—Players dribble about 30 yards, finishing up with a pass on the run.

Station 4: Monkey in the Middle—Three players in a 20-foot square marked off by cones. The monkey tries to steal passes between the other two players. Players should take turns being the monkey.

Station 5: Juggling Practice—Players bounce the ball off different body surfaces.

Place a parent to supervise each station. I'd include other drills on other days, such as:

Triangle Drill—Passing drills between three players where each passes the ball, then runs to a cone to receive the next pass.

Wall Kicking—Players trap the rebound off the wall.

Keep Away—Two teams try consecutive successful passes against each other.

Showdown—Throw the ball between two players and let them charge it.

Dribblemania—Players practice the key dribble moves.

Sharks and Minnows—Each player protects his ball from the "shark."

Half-turns—Players receive the ball with slight contact enough to control the ball as they turn with it.

SPECIALTY SKILLS STATIONS

Station 1: Throw-In Practice—One player does the throw in, while one receives and one defends. Start with form, then work on distance and accuracy, such as throwing to the feet of a teammate on the run.

Station 2: Direct Kicks Practice—Players shoot at the goal over a two-person wall.

Station 3: Heading Practice—Start with players tossing to their own heads, and, after time, have players toss to each other. Move on to header passes to others.

Station 4: Striker Drill—A player serves a centering pass to a striker (center forward) who attempts to score.

Station 5: Corner Kicks—Set up corner kick scenarios to allow practice for a kicker, forward, and goalie.

Each group should stay at each station for five minutes, then rotate all groups among the stations. In twenty-five minutes, each group would have participated in all stations.

During the last forty-five minutes of practice, work on dynamics in scrimmage conditions, stopping when needed to comment on play. Four-on-four games are great, and are probably the best practice kids can have. Six-on-six games allow for the forwards and halfbacks to attack a goal, working out the patterns of a wing attack, center pass, and give and go. Work on corner kicks, making a wall to defend direct kicks, kick-offs, and throw-ins.

If time permits, finish up with a soccer game for fifteen minutes. Divide up all players for a game. Coaches and parents can play too, but remember it's about the kids, so adults should restrain the power of passes. A good approach is to have adults use only the left foot. Always end practice with something fun.

Sometimes we played a variation of baseball/kickball, where players must kick the rolled pitch as hard as they could and circle bases set up in front of a goal. The defending team would need to retrieve the ball, pass toward the goal, and score a goal before the runner got "home." The runner could leave the basepath, retrieve or intercept the ball, and punt it away again, then return to circling the bases. It was hilarious! Always end practice with something fun.

THE PRACTICE PLAN

Each practice should have a written practice plan. It just takes a few minutes to think through what you want to accomplish, and it does wonders for efficient use of time. You can waste a lot of practice time if you are not organized, and you can triple the value of the practice if you are.

Practice plans vary over the course of a season. During the first weeks of practice, add more time for conditioning and individual skills. Then begin to add specialty skills and team dynamics. The best form of practice for kids is small-sided, three-on-three or four-on-four scrimmages. Kids get a lot of touches on the ball, are forced to try to react against pressure and create plays, and get a keen sense of the triangle offense (the use of two teammates nearby to maintain possession and move the ball as a team).

The following are typical sample practice plans for different weeks into the season.

Tuesday Practice Plan

Early birds run a lap. Players pass and trap in pairs, or juggle.

5:30 P.M. Conditioning: Quick cali set, several exercises from the leg stretch set, one from speed drills (Robot, Bounce, Butt-Kick, Goosestep), and one from agility drills set (Simon Says, Carioca).

5:45 P.M. Call team together. Brief comments.

5:50 P.M. Individual Stations: List each station to be used. Parents monitor stations. Five stations, five minutes each.

6:15 P.M. Water break: Five to ten minutes. Use the time to review offensive and defensive concepts.

6:25 P.M. Small-sided game, three on three or four on four, stopping frequently to give instructions. If team is twelve or more players, run two small games.

6:55 P.M. Wind sprints.

7:00 P.M. Closing comments.

Saturday Practice Plan

Early birds run a lap. Players pass and trap in pairs, or juggle.

9:30 A.M. Conditioning: Quick cali set, leg stretch set.

9:40 A.M. Call team together. Brief comments.

9:45 A.M. Individual Stations: Five stations, five minutes each. List skills to be covered.

10:15 A.M. Water break: five to ten minutes. Then continue with stations.

10:25 A.M. Specialty Stations: Three stations, ten minutes each.

10:55 A.M. Full scrimmage.

11:30 A.M. Closing comments.

These plans work well for most age groups. At younger ages, you can shorten the conditioning a bit and spend some time talking soccer. Get the kids in a circle and ask them questions: What's a penalty box? What's a trap? What's a corner kick? Who can name the field positions? What's a free kick? For younger kids, it will take time, but make sure you acquaint the players with every concept.

GAME DAY

As players arrive, have them pair up and do some passing and trapping, as well as some Dribblemania (see page 31) and juggling. Tell the goalies to pair up and toss balls

117

back and forth to each other fairly hard. When all are ready, have a coach or a captain, perhaps a *captain of the day*, lead in some stretching exercises. Then have the team jog a lap around the field. Have them get a drink and call them together to discuss the game. Tell them the line up. Talk about the skills learned in recent practices. Go over who will take corner kicks and direct kicks.

If there is time, have forwards shoot on goal, halfbacks practice passing, and fullbacks do some one-on-one drills. Captains will be called out for a coin toss. If they win, have them choose to defend the goal with the wind at their backs, the down-wind goal, instead of kicking off. Call the team together again for some final encouragement and have them take the field.

During the game, focus on the other team's players. Who is their fastest, most dangerous, forward? You may need to adjust quickly and have a different player defend him or even assign someone specific to mark him one on one. Adjust for any speed mismatches. Where is the weakness in the fullback line? Tell your players to attack through that area. Check your players' positioning and call for them to move up, speed up, or support where needed.

Have a plan for subs worked out before the game starts. Let the kids know generally what it is so they can relax and know when they will go in. Sometimes you will need to adjust and let them know what you are doing. Have an assistant coach keep game time and remind you to get the subs in.

At halftime, get the team to a spot away from everyone and talk about the half. Check and see how everyone feels. Check to see if anyone is exhausted from the heat. Be sure the kids drink plenty of water. Typically, a team "parent for the day" buys oranges. Be positive. Get them up to casually stretch again a bit before the halftime ends.

During the second half, observe your players for fatigue. If you can substitute, give rest to the ones who need it most. In a close game, ensure your first team is rested and on the field for the final four minutes.

Win or lose, the kids need to leave the field feeling good. Praise effort. Accentuate the positives. Avoid long meetings after a game; save it for the next practice.

INJURIES

The most common injuries in soccer are sprains. After ankle sprains, medial collateral ligament (MCL) and anterior cruciate ligament (ACL) sprains are most common. Knees are tough injuries. Often the injury will require some sort of arthroscopic surgery to mend cartilage. Modern procedures are quite advanced and simple. Have your child see a knowledgeable sports doctor. Your team's coach or high school athletic director will know one. The sharp pivoting, stopping, and lateral movements of soccer significantly contribute to these injuries.

As suggested, a good warm-up routine and stretches will help prevent some sprains. Also, to avoid risk, check out the field for holes, ruts, glass, or obstacles before playing. If a sprain does occur in the ankle or wrist, it should be immobilized. An ice pack should be applied immediately. Broken bones are rare, but not rare enough. Act as if there is a fracture until you're sure there is no fracture. If there is a fracture, immobilize the child completely as soon as possible—no movement at all. Be comforting, keep the player warm, and get medical help. Do not allow your child to be moved or cared for by anyone who is not medically trained. If in the middle of the field during a game, the game can wait. Insist on this. Permanent damage can result from aggravating a break. The child should get an X-ray.

The most common muscle strains in soccer occur with groin muscles, hamstrings, and quadriceps. A muscle strain won't require emergency care, but will get very sore and need a few days rest. Again, these strains occur frequently in soccer given the constant stop-and-go movement. Bloody noses and bruises are also common to youth soccer.

Other common injuries fall into the category of *overuse injuries*, arising from repeated or prolonged athletic use of the limbs, especially near the end of a long season. These injuries are the result of repeated pressure and overloading of a tendon, muscle, bone, or joint, resulting in its breakdown. Osgood-Schlatter disease, also known as growing pains, is a painful bump in the kneecap or shin bone. This can become inflamed by repetitive running or jumping. Any child with this problem should see a physician and get an appropriate amount of rest.

Abrasions usually occur when a child falls and scrapes the side of the leg. They are the most likely cuts to get infected. Wash the wound as soon as possible, with soap if handy. Apply a sterile dressing when you are able to, the sooner the better. If you have it, put some antiseptic ointment on the cut. If the wound gets red or pussy, or red tracks appear, the child should see a physician immediately.

Lacerations are deeper wounds. Unless bleeding is severe, wash the wound, and apply slight pressure with a bandage to stop the bleeding. If severe, seek professional help. In the meantime, apply pressure and a large bandage. Immediately elevate the wound higher than the heart to slow bleeding. If the bandage gets blood-soaked, apply another on top of it. Don't remove the first one. Care for shock by elevating the

119

legs unless you suspect a head or neck injury. In this case, don't move the child. If the laceration is minor, a butterfly bandage will hold the skin together. Consult a physician immediately if you suspect stitches are needed.

Contusions and bruises occur frequently, even through shin guards. Apply ice quickly, after handling any abrasion or lacerations. Ice will arrest internal bleeding and prevent or lessen swelling. Ice is the best treatment to have available for nearly any swelling from bruises or sprains. Apply it very quickly, within minutes, and much internal damage will be spared.

If a child ever falls to the ground unconscious, send for an ambulance and see if there is a doctor, paramedic, or anyone trained as a first responder available. The first move, once it is clear that the child will not respond, is to check for vital signs—breathing and pulse. If either are missing, have someone who has been certified administer rescue breathing or cardiopulmonary resuscitation (CPR). Try to stay calm and let the medical workers do their job. In all my years of coaching four sports, and playing even more, I've never seen CPR needed. I hope you won't either.

Finally, heat exhaustion can occur easily during a soccer match. The body gets clammy and pale. Remove the child from the game and get him into the shade or a cool spot. Apply cool towels to the back of the neck, forehead, and wrists and elevate the feet. If the body temperature is very high and the pupils are constricted, you should suspect heat stroke. Call an ambulance and cool the child down fast. Care for shock.

Tell your child to play the game safely. Aggressiveness is okay, but be careful not to hurt someone. Your hope is that other parents do the same.

When injury occurs, insist on rest. I've seen many kids rush back from a sprained ankle, only to have the injury plague them through the years. Don't let it happen. Make sure your child wears a brace to protect him from any further aggravation or injury.

Injuries need time to heal properly. If you give the proper time, your child will be able to participate in sports for many years. If you don't, it could be over already.

ON PEAK PERFORMANCE

The bane of coaches is whatever it is that makes a kid play great one day and completely fall apart the next.

Modern science tells us that how we cope with the stress of a challenge before us is largely mental—it's all upstairs. Mental control begins with the *fight or flight* instinct, that is, the natural impulse that arises in cornered animals to respond to a threat by fighting it or fleeing from it. It is a genetic reaction, inherited by humans from their earliest ancestors. There's not a kid alive who hasn't felt those butterflies in the stomach. This reaction under game conditions can create a panic that distracts concentration and even causes muscle spasm. However, when controlled properly, it can lead the athlete to a *zone* of peak performance.

STEPS TO IMPROVE PEAK PERFORMANCE

Research suggests several steps coaches can take to create or strive for the conditions optimal to peak performance.

Coaches have already done some of this for years. The time-honored best way to produce a controlled response to game-day excitement is constant repetition during practice. Much of this book deals with the need to repeatedly practice dribbling and passing, including adherence to proper form. This is so game responses become automatic and can occur even if the player is under stress or too excited.

Studies also suggest that a ritual-like approach to game day is conducive to a relaxed state of mind. A regular pattern of eating, exercise, dressing, and pre-game discussion is highly recommended. Try to avoid any surprises or deviations.

Sports psychologists have long supported mental imaging of athletic routines. Olympic athletes have been tracing their steps mentally for years. What we have now are clear scientific bases for these approaches. These techniques are useful at all levels of play. They are perhaps most needed at the youngest levels where kids cannot control the anxieties of competition.

Premature arousal of adrenalin hours before the game can result in the level in the blood dropping after a few hours, even to a point below normal at game time. This will lead to subpar performance and is another reason to have relaxed, stable pre-game routines. Some coaches now employ Zen-type meditations in the training programs, providing athletes with methods to evoke relaxed states of mind at will.

Many coaches have some concept they use to focus players on achieving peak performance. I always tell my players to try to get an edge over their opponent. We talk about how evenly matched most good teams usually are, and that the winner will be the team who has some edge over the opponent. This concept helps me to get kids to accept the idea of improving their mental approach as one way to get an edge.

121

WHAT KIND OF COACH WILL YOU BE?

08

The relationship between a coach and a player is a powerful one. You are not only an authority figure, but you are in full control over what is, in the player's mind, the most important thing in life.

Through athletic experiences, a kid finds out about himself—good or bad—and he will always associate those things with you. Coaching is an awesome responsibility.

You may want to ignore this larger picture, but sticking your head in the sand doesn't change your responsibility for making a positive and lasting impact on players. This book provides many tools you can use to help you make the experience a good one, regardless of whether you win or lose as a team.

Most of your players will never make cuts at the high-school level, few will may play in college, and you will likely never coach a future pro soccer player. However, every one of your players will become an adult someday, with the responsibility of a job and probably a family as well.

The whole idea of youth sports is to provide life lessons. I define coaching as the challenge of inspiring a child to know she can draw something greater from herself in the effort to succeed. That's the mission, and all else flows from that purpose. It's all about the kids and helping them to become better athletes and better people.

It is doubtful that your players will remember much about this season twenty years from now, certainly not the scores of games. But I guarantee you one thing: *They will remember you for the rest of their lives*.

The memories of my coaches are etched clearly in my mind. I remember them vividly, for good or for bad. You may not remember all of the kids you coach, particularly if you do it for a number of years, but every one of them will remember you. How will you be remembered?

Our society is ferociously competitive in spirit. Pressuring children too hard may turn them into adults so obsessed with being first that they get no joy out of life except in the narrow field of competition. They never give nor get pleasure in their relationships with spouses, children, friends, and fellow workers.

— *Dr. Benjamin Spock*

08

We have all seen the ugly side of youth sports. We have seen parents pressuring their kids to the point of belittling them. We've seen the kids so driven by their need to succeed that they never find real joy in athletic endeavors, just relief when they don't fail.

The debate about competition is quite fierce with extreme views on each side: Some say never keep score; others point to the reality of competition throughout life. Let's face it, if you tell kids that winning is not important, they may nod passively, but they are not going to buy it. They know about winning. They know the kids on the other team will gloat and taunt them back in the neighborhood or at school. They know all about trophies and news articles. They hear the empty silence after a loss, or worse, the criticism from the coach or their parents.

Well, as with so many things in life, both sides have some truth, depending on the situation. Sure, kids do talk about winning, for a few moments just before they head for the pool. But I believe what will last with kids deep down is how they feel about how well they are personally doing, and this feeling they will get from coaches and parents as much as anyone else. What kids will remember is how they felt about themselves and how you reacted.

Competition stirs up some powerful emotions, and if the coach can't handle his emotions, the kids will follow suit. It's said that winning builds character, while losing reveals it. At the heart of how good a coach or parent you are is how well you balance your need to win with the need to develop healthy young people. Whether and how you strike that balance will affect your every action, your relationship with each player, and the atmosphere on the field. It will surely characterize the memory of your coaching experience for many years to come. Striking that balance involves a continuing struggle between those passions fired up by competition and the caring you feel for your players as a responsible adult. The moment of truth is at the peak of competition in a close game or after a loss. What is the image your players see at that moment? Are you in control, reassuring, calling for their best? Or are you screaming, critical, or angry?

124

Admittedly, winning is important in professional sports. And maybe it becomes important even for some kids in high school, since college coaches will overlook a kid on a team with a 3-15 record. But in youth sports, especially for beginners, it's just not important in the least.

I tell my kids something they can believe—that winning is never important, but that it is always fun. That's the truth. They can relate to it. I tell them it's important to try to be as good as they can be, to help each other, and to try to do their best. We surely try to win, but all we can really control is how hard we try. What's important is how they handle victory or defeat.

I often find that balance in light of how much talent I have on a team. When I see that we have little chance of winning it all, then I choose to emphasize individual goals. Let's face it, if you can't get there, there is absolutely no sense in getting everyone crazy. But when you have a potential championship team … that's the real test. How do you give them their best chance at success on the field, while ensuring that the overall experience is positive and builds character?

I recently read in the *New York Times* that some schools are abandoning competitive interaction in their physical education programs to avoid damaging the feelings of kids who are not outstanding. Isn't it better for kids to learn about and prepare for success and failure in a controlled setting, inside the relatively harmless gymnasium, than in the crucible of adult life? Should we abandon competition as a society? We couldn't quit if we wanted to. It's part of life and we just need to continue to work to find the best balance.

Winning and growth do share common ground. Coaches who win consistently often are remembered by their former players more for the great lessons of life than for the gold cup on the mantel. They know that the key to success is in knowing how to motivate athletes to win the personal struggle to do their best, to improve beyond their limits, spurred on by their team's goals. They know that the spirit, the will to win, and the will to excel transcend the game itself.

How you resolve the balance between winning and individual development is up to you. If you just recognize the need to strike a balance, you are off to a good start.

My own approach in coaching is probably best characterized as a back-and-forth struggle around that balance. I think it's enough to be honest about the reality of competitive passion and then commit ourselves as coaches to doing what we expect of our players, doing our best with it. I believe most coaches want to build character and a positive experience for each player, while trying to win the game.

08

Some coaches never really challenge their team for fear of upsetting the kids, and these "nice guys" don't do much damage. Of course, their players may never make it to the next level of play. Other coaches, at the opposite extreme, feel compelled to win at all costs, and the cost can be tragic for the fragile psyche of a young boy or girl. Find the middle ground. If you find you can't deal with the pressure, then consider whether coaching is right for you and for the kids.

The practical way to get a reality check is to pick out a parent who seems to know the other parents well, and ask her how things seem to be going. Parents talk to each other about how they feel and how their kids are feeling, and you can learn things a parent would never tell you directly. Get some feedback on how you are doing.

Of course, the issues vary with the age of your team. At preteen levels, the emphasis is always heavily on developing the individual. This doesn't mean that winning is not an issue, it's just not all-important. The focus is solely on development. This is why most programs require that all kids play a certain amount of time. By the time of high school varsity play, winning takes on more importance, but creating a positive experience is still essential. Winning should never completely take precedence over the positive experience. But the reality of major collegiate play is that losing coaches don't last.

ON MOTIVATION

> Rock, I know I'm going to die. I'm not afraid. But someday, Rock,
> when things on the field are going against us, tell the boys, Rock,
> to go out there and win just one for the Gipper. Now, I don't know
> where I'll be then, coach. But I'll know about it, and I'll be happy.
> — George Gipp

Okay, it's a football story (American football, that is), but it's the best motivational story there is. Legendary Notre Dame coach Knute Rockne waited eight years until, during halftime in a big game against Army, he repeated these last words of his dying quarterback in what was to become the epitome of halftime motivation.

It's a beautiful story, but coaches need more than speeches and a charismatic personality to motivate their team. There are ways that *all* coaches can motivate their players.

ATTAWAY!

There never will be a better tool for young athletes than frequent positive reinforcement. It is essential to liberally give out "attaboys" or "attagirls" for good effort. In *Kidsports: A*

Survival Guide for Parents, Dr. Nathan J. Smith, a consultant for the American Board of Pediatrics, reported on his study of two groups of coaches. He found that "the single most important difference in our research between coaches to whom young athletes respond most favorably and those to whom they respond least favorably was the frequency with which coaches reinforce and reward desirable behavior." A pat on the back, a smile, clapping, praise, a wink and a nod, as well as tangible rewards, such as mention in a newspaper article or more playing time—all go a very long way toward motivating high performance. I would add that the rewards are even more effective when they emphasize outstanding effort as opposed to a great result. An athlete has complete control over the amount of effort he puts into his game, but the result depends on many things, many of which are beyond the individual's control. Even corrective action, such as pointing out mistakes, should be sandwiched somehow within some positive comments, such as "Good try, Jack. Next time keep your head up. You can do it!"

Coaches spend a lot of time hollering, trying to motivate players, trying to get them to increase their energy level, and trying to develop that all-important desire to perform. However, there is a line that shouldn't be crossed: Never humiliate a player. The idea is to be firm, to let players know that they are capable of doing better if they reach deeper into their gut. But let them know that you believe in them and their abilities, too.

Having one set of standards for everyone doesn't mean you shouldn't handle players differently. Some kids respond well when you correct them in front of their peers. Others are devastated when you criticize them, even if done calmly and constructively. You will quickly get a feel for this from their reaction to you. Take these kids aside and explain what you saw. Some kids will seem troubled all the time, so sit down with them and find out what's going on in their lives; see if you can learn what the problem is.

At advanced levels, your expectations for performance are much higher. Players will generally have the skills, and it is the lapses in concentration that most affect performance. Yelling will get a kid's attention, but it will also humiliate him. There is a way to get his attention and still be positive. As noted earlier, the essence of coaching is to inspire an athlete to be all he can be, and thus coaching criticism must be grounded in the notion that the player can do better.

Let a player know what you think about his effort, not him as a person. Don't personalize it. The kid is a decent person, it's the effort you want more of, so focus on the effort during practice. A kid can relate to trying harder, but he can't relate positively to you telling him he stinks. Explain the problem with fundamentals or form so that he understands the concept. Work with him until he gets the idea.

08

Most important: Reward good effort openly and liberally. Praise a good pass. Recognize hustle. Yell out, "That's soccer!" It can get infectious.

WE ARE FAMILY

I've read the autobiographies of many great coaches. One constant in all of their stories is their ability to relate to the different individuals on their team, to create a family-type environment.

Each kid is different, whether on a team or in a family, and each one needs a personal approach. Even the weakest players should be treated with the same respect as the best players.

I start each season with a team discussion on what it means to be on a team. One thing I tell the players is that, for the rest of the season, they are all friends. They are all in a special relationship with each other. I tell them they should say hello in the school hallways and help each other out, off the field, if needed. I never tolerate criticism of a teammate on the field and quickly bench any offender. I expect kids to urge each other on, to quickly tell a teammate to put a mistake behind him. I promote team dinners and outings and move to break up cliques.

Team building is a proven ticket to success. The concept is widely used in all walks of life and is a staple of business organization. Team building doesn't just happen because a bunch of kids are on a team. It happens because coaches work at it. It's actually quite easy to get done. Just put it in the practice plan, and talk to your assistant coaches about it. Opportunities to promote team unity will present themselves in abundance.

DON'T UNDERESTIMATE YOUR KIDS

Aren't kids too young to learn all this? Well, if your players are very young, then it will be a while before the more complex skills will be understood well enough to routinely occur on the field. But all of it—including the more complicated concepts—should be taught, or at least started, at all ages. Don't underestimate your players. Some of them will grasp these concepts. The basics should be emphasized right away before bad habits form. If parents and coaches set the stage in early years, some of the advanced concepts might click by age ten. But if your players are green, don't worry about it. Concentrate on the basics, and go over the advanced stuff, but don't expect too much too soon.

Believe me when I say there is no magic age for mastering soccer skills. Look at the age of kids mastering moves in gymnastics. It's not that younger kids can't learn.

They just need someone who understands refined concepts and has the time and ability to teach them. A lot depends on how much time you have to practice.

There isn't anything in this book that's over the heads of young kids. Just start somewhere, and the kids will absorb as much as you have the time and patience to teach them. Some skills will take a few sessions, some will require much more, and some will take years, but eventually, it will all come together. Like learning how to whistle, one day it's suddenly there, and you sense it was always really simple to do.

ON PARENTS

Parents can be a great help in youth sports; however, interfering parents can be a major problem for coaches. This is especially true in soccer because parents are usually right on top of the team, so their complaining is more visible.

I have no problem with parents who, after the game, want to talk to the coach and find out whether there is some issue they need to be aware of. But, often, they are argumentative and even downright insulting. Of course, you don't need to take abuse from any parent. But before you get too defensive, think about what's going on.

Most parents die a little bit when they see their child going through a bad time. Maybe their child is not playing much or is having self-doubts, and she's acting out at home or school because of it. This may not be something that is evident at practice, but it involves you as the coach. Maybe you can get some insight into what is troubling the child. Parents feel the pain along with their kids, and they may be emotional when they confront you. Hear them out.

There also may be a problem with the child that the parent isn't aware of. Give them some ideas to help them understand what the problem is, and perhaps you can pinpoint some things they can do to help their child. Tell them you are nudging the kid because you think he can do better, and you are trying to arouse his potential.

Maybe you are dead wrong and need to give the kid another look. Tell the parents you will consider what they said. I've seen kids who sat on the bench as a sub for half a season suddenly come alive and wind up starting the rest of the games.

Most of all, keep in mind that you're talking about their kid. Parents may feel a bit threatened by your control over their child. As a parent, I have had uneasy feelings about coaches—it's quite natural. A little patience on your part can defuse some strong emotions. You can turn a potential feud into something that helps the child and, ultimately, the team.

On the other hand, parents who abuse their children during a game are a major problem. These are the parents who scorn their children for a bad pass or missed goal. I've seen parents complain loudly about their daughter sitting out while a less skilled child gets playing time. It's the worst thing in sports to see. You do not have to put up with this. Talk to such parents and ask them to keep quiet. If they don't, remove them from the field. In one instance, when I asked a parent who was loudly criticizing his child to leave, he threatened me with removing his son as well. My response was that I hoped he wouldn't, but that his son not playing was better than what was going on, and that it would not continue under my watch. The parent stayed home; the kid played.

I rarely have problems with parents. When you can achieve a certain level of team spirit, negativity gets left behind. I always seek to empower parents by getting them involved with the team in some manner: as assistant coaches, as practice aids who shag errant kicks and help with water breaks, as fund drive chairs, or as administrators of other tasks like uniform distribution or starting phone trees to pass on information. Delegate as much as possible, and you'll bring parents into the team dynamic.

NOTES FOR PARENTS

How to Act at Games

The worst thing that you can do is go to a soccer game and scream your head off. I have seen groups of parents by the sidelines screaming at the players, giving directions, and generally raising a ruckus. The scene is all too common: Some poor kid is running up to a loose ball, and parents are screaming, "Get the ball! Get the ball!" Believe me, the kid already knows that. Unfortunately, the screaming focuses his mind more on the ball, when he really needs to be looking around at whom to pass to. Actually, it's best just to congratulate nice play and be quiet. The kids on the field or the coach should be communicating to the player about the options. A lot of screaming parents telling players what to do is just confusing. Sometimes the referee will caution against sideline coaching.

If you can't contain yourself, then try to say things that will be helpful. Messages must be clear and concise. For instance, if your child is dribbling and a defender approaches from the rear, yell, "Man on." If they tend to bunch up, remind them to spread out.

Most important, be positive. Don't criticize anyone, especially your child. Don't take out your frustrations on the kid who makes a mistake. It embarrasses both of you, and it only teaches the child to play with less confidence. I guarantee they will all make

130

mistakes, for years, and they will not improve if you punctuate mistakes with things like, "What's the matter with you?" or "That was stupid!" If you cannot control yourself, stay home. This may sound tough, but you will do a lot of damage to your child and to your relationship with your child if you don't control anger.

How to Treat the Coach

First of all, the coach is giving up a lot of time. He's put in the most time, so he has the most voice. If you want to coach, sign up or volunteer to help at practices. That earns you the right to have an opinion. Otherwise, be very conservative about offering it.

Second, realize your bias. You are a parent who loves your child. You may think he deserves to play more or to play another position. But the coach knows a lot more about what the kids can do and who has earned playing time. It's unfair for you to ask for more, and unfair to the other kids to suggest that one of them should play less. Work more with your child and foster improvement and more playing time will follow. Coaches want to win, and they usually will give the better players more playing time.

However, coaches need to learn too, and sometimes they go about things the wrong way. If this is the case, gently indicate how you feel. It's important that you think about the situation a lot and make sure you know what you're talking about before you speak to him. Question your own biases. If you feel you can help, offer your opinion about it. Avoid an argument. Make your point and ask the coach to think about it. Indicate you are only trying to help. Listen to the coach's response, then thank him for his time and end it. If you're lucky, the coach will be thankful, but he may resent your interference and possibly even take it out on your child. If the situation becomes very bad, let someone in your soccer organization know what is happening. Keep in mind that your child may suffer if caught in the middle. If the experience is more damaging than good, remove your child from the team. But remember to think about it, get advice, talk to other parents, and avoid being unnecessarily disruptive.

COACHES' AND PARENTS' CHECKLIST

Now that you have read the book, it's time to get outside and have some fun with your child. I find it useful when I coach to have a checklist of things I want to remember during practice, so here is a checklist for you to use. Keep saying these things over and over.

DRIBBLING

- ☐ Use both feet.
- ☐ Keep the eyes up.
- ☐ Sweep the ball; do not strike it.
- ☐ Keep it close for control.
- ☐ Maintain body balance.
- ☐ Use head and body fakes.
- ☐ Explode to open space.

JUGGLING

- ☐ Use feet, thigh, head, and chest.
- ☐ Concentrate on the bottom of the ball.
- ☐ Don't juggle too high at first.
- ☐ Do one better each time.

PASSING

- ☐ Know where your nearest teammates are.
- ☐ Pass in front of the receiver with appropriate ball speed.
- ☐ Settle the ball down before passing.

133

☐ Hop and plant the non-kicking foot at the side of the ball.

☐ Keep the knee over the ball, point the toe down, and lock the ankle.

☐ Use inside, outside, or instep depending on direction and distance from the target.

☐ Snap leg for more speed.

☐ Follow through.

☐ Move on contact.

RECEIVING THE PASS

☐ Get to the ball.

☐ Meet the ball; don't wait for it.

☐ Take command of the ball.

☐ Face the ball and present a body surface.

☐ Relax upon contact.

☐ Deaden surface and withdraw.

☐ Decide where to drop the ball; know where the defender is.

☐ Volley if need be.

☐ Move on contact.

THROW-INS

☐ Try to throw it up along the sideline.

☐ Be ready for a pass back.

☐ Throw forward, from over the head, with both hands evenly in one motion, with both feet on the ground.

☐ Drag back toe if needed to keep contact with the ground.

HEADING

☐ Concentrate, keep the eyes open.

☐ Make contact with the forehead.

☐ Neck rigid, body balanced.

☐ Arch back and thrust head to pass.

☐ Jump for high balls; hinge waist.

OFFENSIVE CONCEPTS

- ☐ Attack from the wings.
- ☐ Spread the field.
- ☐ Overlap and support.
- ☐ Use triangulation.
- ☐ Flow with the ball.
- ☐ Move off the ball.
- ☐ Square and pass to center.
- ☐ Switch positions.
- ☐ Encourage shots.
- ☐ Communicate.

DEFENSIVE CONCEPTS

- ☐ Challenge the ball.
- ☐ Contain and apply pressure, but don't overcommit.
- ☐ Cover and support.
- ☐ Keep the ball away from the middle.
- ☐ Mark free players.
- ☐ Don't hang around goal.
- ☐ Use offside traps.
- ☐ Don't kick into an opposing player.
- ☐ Tackle before a player has control.
- ☐ Clear when in trouble.
- ☐ Pass to goalie if needed.
- ☐ Make a wall on free kicks.
- ☐ Communicate.

GLOSSARY: TALKING SOCCER

One of the important tasks of coaching a beginner team is to discuss the terminology of soccer so the kids know the basic terms. Take a few minutes at each practice and go over a list of words. The following glossary, "Talking Soccer," covers the main rules in detail and much of the language of the game. I've already covered much of the game in preceding chapters so I will not duplicate everything here.

Advantage: The referee may disregard a foul and allow play to continue if the fouled team has possession and would be disadvantaged by stoppage of play.

Ballside: On defense, positioning oneself between an opponent without the ball and the ball, (i.e., on the ballside of the opponent).

Bicycle Kick: A fancy play where a player falls backward kicking the ball when upside down to a point behind him. It is a dangerous move for players lacking experience.

Breakaway: When a striker or wing forward breaks away from a defender and charges the goalie one on one, creating an excellent scoring opportunity.

Cards: Referees carry a yellow and a red card, which they will flash upon a serious foul. The yellow card is a caution, signaling that another similar infraction will lead to an ejection. An intentional flagrant foul that may cause injury is immediately met with a red card and an ejection from the game. The team must play without the full amount of players.

Carry: Another word for dribbling.

Center Pass: A pass toward the center of the field in front of the goal. It's the bread-and-butter play of soccer offense.

Center Circle: A 10-yard radius circle in the middle of the field where play starts at the beginning of each half and after each goal. Defenders may not enter the circle until the ball rolls one full turn.

Center Line: The line that divides the field in half, parallel to the goal lines.

Clear: A hard defensive kick, clearing the ball from the area in front of the goal. This is usually a desperation kick to no one in particular, when under pressure.

Contain: An effort to slow down an opponent's advance or restrict an opponent's movement.

Corner Kick: Whenever the ball goes out of bounds past the goal line and was last touched by a defensive player, the opponent is awarded a free direct kick. The ball is placed within a small pie-shaped area with a 1-yard radius, at the corner of the field nearest to where the ball went out of bounds. The offensive player kicks the ball and tries to place it near the goal.

Charge: The shoulder charge is a legal play, jarring the player with the ball, so long as the arm does not touch the player, and so long as one is playing the ball upon contact. If too hard or dangerous, the referee will award a free kick.

Direct Kick: A direct kick means that the kicker may score by shooting directly at the goal. Direct kicks are awarded upon intentional fouls such as kicking, jumping, striking, tripping, holding, pushing another player, or intentionally touching the ball with the hand or arm.

Distribute: Usually used to describe the goalie's effort to pass or punt the ball to a teammate. It can also reference a midfield pass.

Dink: Originally a volleyball term, it's a soft chip shot over a charging goalie's head.

Drop Ball: This does not occur often, but when the referee does not know who last touched the ball out of bounds, or after an injury during play, play begins again with a drop ball, similar to the face-off in hockey. The ball is dropped between two players and all others must stay 10 yards away.

Far Post: The goalpost farthest from the shooter and the goalie. Aiming shots at the far post allows for a second-chance shot by teammates if the first one misses. It also allows more time for the ball to curve into the goal.

Flags: Flags that are at least 5 feet high used to mark the four corners of the field.

Forwards: Offensive players that often shoot on the goal. They are fast, good dribblers, and can shoot or pass on the run. The forward positions are wing forwards, center forward, and inside forwards. They can also be called strikers.

Free Kicks: Goal kicks, penalty kicks, corner kicks, and direct and indirect kicks, awarded upon various violations.

Fullbacks: Defensive players that are big, strong, and aggressive. The fullback positions are wing fullbacks, center fullback, sweeper, and stopper.

Give-and-Go Pass: An essential offensive maneuver involving a short pass to a team-mate and a quick pass back as the first player sprints past the defender. Also called a *wall pass*.

Goal Box: The small box area in front of the goal, usually extending about 6 yards from the goal line. The ball must be placed within the goal box for a goal kick.

Goal Kick: A free kick awarded to the defense when an offensive player kicks the ball out of bounds beyond the goal line. It must be taken from within the goal area on the side from which the ball went out of bounds. The ball must exit the penalty area before any player can play it.

Handball: If a player deliberately handles the ball (meaning to touch the ball with the hand or with the arm up to just below the shoulder), the team loses possession. The opponent is awarded a direct free kick. It can also lead to a yellow or red card.

Halfbacks: Players who cover the middle of the field. They have good skills and are endurance runners. The halfback positions are wing halfbacks and center halfback. Halfbacks are also known as midfielders or linkmen.

Indirect Kick: A kick awarded for unintentional fouls, obstruction, or dangerous play such as raising the foot high, dangerously lowering one's head, unsportsmanlike be-havior, abusive language, kicking the ball when on the ground, or kicking a ball held by the goalie. On an indirect kick, another player must touch the ball before a goal can be scored.

Kickoff: The opening kick of each soccer half and after each score. The opposing players must remain outside the center circle until the ball has advanced forward a distance equal to the ball's circumference. A typical kickoff has two forwards in the circle; one rolls it to the other who then kicks the ball back to the center halfback, who then kicks up to a wing for a possible wing attack. Defensive players, especially halfbacks, should pick up any wings who penetrate their area during a kickoff and anticipate the pass. (See figure 1–2 on page 10.)

Linesman: Officials who roam the sidelines with a small flag in hand to signal the referee when the ball goes out of bounds, or when they see an offside or other infraction. The final call is the referee's. They are more often referred to as assistant referees. Usually you will not see them until high school or championship play.

Mark: To defend against a particular person, to stay close by him. This *must* be done to any offensive player in the penalty area. Also called man-to-man defense.

Midfield: The middle third of a soccer field.

Move off the Ball: Getting into position to help the team when one does not have possession of the ball; to try to run to or create open space.

Near Post: The goalpost nearest the ball.

Obstruction: Impeding the movement of an opponent if one is not within playing distance of the ball. This is a penalty, and the opponent is awarded an indirect kick.

Offside: The rule books say that a player is offside if nearer the opponent's goal line than the ball is at the moment the ball is played toward the player by a teammate, unless a) the player is on one's own half of the field; or b) two defenders (including the goalie) are nearer the goal line than the attacker; or c) the offensive player receives the ball on a goal kick, corner kick, throw-in, or drop ball. This all means that offensive players cannot just hang around the opposing goalie, waiting for a pass. They have to have the ball, or a defender plus the goalie has to be inside them. Players basically have to *earn* forward progress with the ball. Defenders can use this rule effectively to stop forwards from penetrating.

One-Touch: To trap the ball and immediately pass it with the next touch.

Overlap: Movement of players past other teammates to receive a pass, in order to advance the ball.

Penalty: Any violation of a rule of the game. Upon a violation, the referee may stop play. (See Referee Signals on page 141.) However, if the team violated has possession

REFEREE SIGNALS

141

of the ball, the referee may allow them the *advantage*. This means the referee thinks it's better for them to play on than to receive a free kick. When play is blown dead, the referee signals whether the award is a *direct kick*, by pointing his hand toward goal, or an *indirect kick*, by pointing his hand straight up. The referee's other hand usually points to the spot where the kick must be taken. Defensive players must stand 10 yards away from the kicker on all free kicks. If close to the goal the defense often forms a human wall to protect the goal.

Penalty Kick: A kick awarded for a violation within the penalty area that would result in a direct kick. The shot is taken from a point 12 yards from the center of the goal. All other players must remain outside the penalty area. The goalie must have both feet on the goal line until the ball is kicked. The kicker or a teammate may take additional shots upon a rebound touched by the goalie (a rebound off the goalpost not touched by the goalie is a dead ball).

Penalty Mark: A mark 12 yards from the goal line from where penalty kicks are made.

Recover: The transition to defense, to get back goalside, especially if the ball is nearer the goal and defenders need support.

Settle: To control the ball after receiving a hard pass.

Serve: To pass the ball.

Shootout: If a game ends in a tie, each team selects five players to alternately shoot on goal from the penalty mark. The team with the most goals wins. If still tied after all ten kicks, the shooting continues with different players in sudden death.

Shin Guards: Fiberglass shield guards that protect the shins from injuries and broken bones.

Slide Tackle: Sliding to tackle the ball from a player. It is a desperation move used when an opponent has beaten a player to the ball. Missing the ball and hitting the player may lead to a penalty.

Small-Sided Game: A practice game of between three to six players on a side, usually played sideways on the field, using cones spaced 4–6 feet apart as goals. A good rule, since there is no goalie, is that the ball must travel below knee height when scoring. Beginners should never play more than five on a side, because the larger numbers overwhelm them.

Soccer Ball Sizes: Soccer balls come in three basic sizes. Size 5 is the primary official regulation, and is 27–28 inches in circumference, about an inch in diameter smaller than a basketball, and 14–16 ounces in weight. Size 4 is smaller by a few inches and few ounces, and is used for kids below twelve years of age. Size 3 is for tiny tots. The ball should always be properly inflated, otherwise it could lead to injury.

Square: To make a lateral pass to a teammate infield of the passer.

Tackle: To steal the ball from a dribbler.

Through Pass: A pass past the defense for a teammate, usually a wing, to run to.

Tiebreaker: A relatively recent innovation employed to break ties, usually in a championship match where there must be a winner. Sometimes there is extended play; other times there is a *shootout*. If a tie remains after the shootout, the teams do a sudden death kick where the first to score wins.

Trap: To receive a pass or otherwise collect a moving ball.

Two-Touch: To trap the ball and then allow one dribble before passing.

Volley: Kicking a ball in midair.

Wall: A line of defenders, shoulder to shoulder, who deflect a free kick.

Wall Pass: *See give and go.*

INDEX

145

149